ANNE FRANK

CENTENNIAL BOOKS

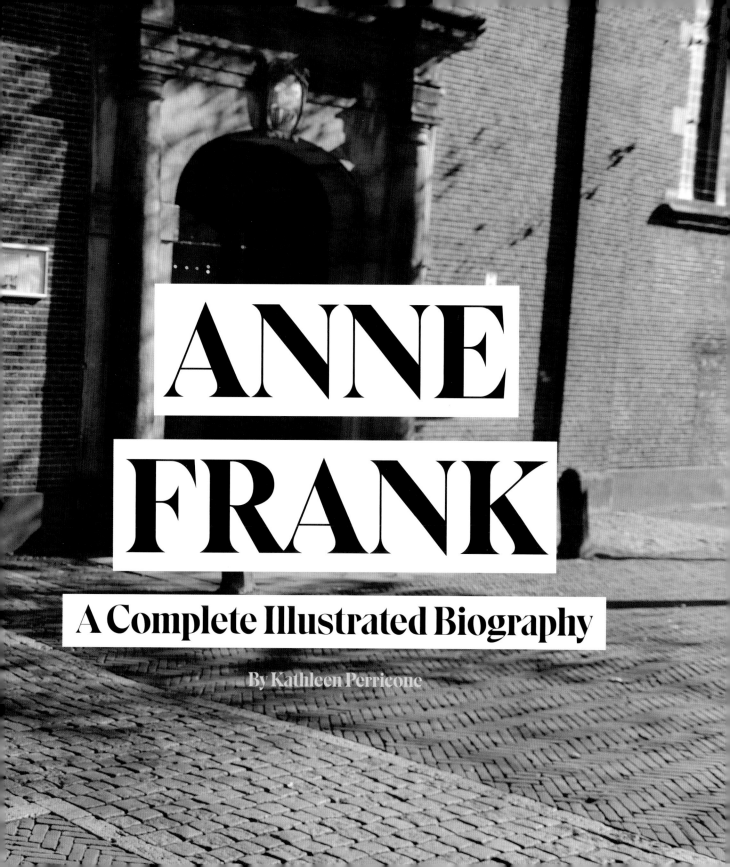

ANNE FRANK

A Complete Illustrated Biography

By Kathleen Perricone

Uitgang / Exit →
Garderobe / Cloak room →

Visitors can reflect on Anne's experience in person at the Anne Frank House in Amsterdam.

CONTENTS

6 | FOREWORD
Laureen Nussbaum, Anne's childhood friend, reflects on how the diary still resonates today.

Chapter 1 Early Life

10 | "I WAS BORN HAPPY"
Anne's earliest years were enjoyably spent amid friends and family in her German home.

Chapter 2 Nazi Threat

26 | RUNNING FROM HITLER
The dictator's rise to power forced the Franks to flee their home and head to relative safety in Holland.

36 | NAZIS ARRIVE IN AMSTERDAM
With the German invasion, the family faced an imminent threat to their very survival.

38 | NO JEWS ALLOWED
The Nazi occupation led to severe restrictions for Dutch Jews, and that was only the beginning.

46 | AS FRIENDS KNEW HER
Childhood companions share their fond memories of young Anne.

54 | DEAR DIARY
The 13th birthday present that changed Anne's life—and history.

Chapter 3 Into Hiding

64 | RACE FOR REFUGE
At dawn, the Franks made a mad dash for the Secret Annex in an effort to outrun the Nazis.

70 | WHO WERE THE HELPERS?
The trusted employees who were responsible for the Franks' survival.

74 | LIFE IN SECRET
How the fugitives passed 761 long days and nights.

84 | TOUR THE ANNEX
A closer look at life inside 263 Prinsengracht.

86 | SISTER RIVALRY
Shifting emotions brought tension to Anne and Margot's relationship.

Chapter 4 Found Out

94 | DISCOVERED BY THE NAZIS
An informant's tip led the Gestapo right to the Secret Annex.

106 | LAST TRAIN TO AUSCHWITZ
After a short time, the Franks were sent to the infamous death camp.

114 | ALONE TOGETHER
Away from their parents, the sisters leaned on each other in their final months of suffering.

Chapter 5 Searching for Answers

126 | "WHAT HAPPENED TO MARGOT AND ANNE?"
Otto desperately sought out answers about his daughters' fates.

134 | OTTO FINDS LOVE AGAIN
How the bereaved widower found consolation with a fellow survivor.

140 | UNSOLVED MYSTERY
Who betrayed Anne? A team of investigators search for the truth.

Chapter 6 Anne's Legacy

154 | DIARY DRAMA
A childhood friend advocates for the publication of Anne's real text.

162 | HOLLYWOOD ENDING
From Broadway to the big screen and beyond, how Anne's diary and legacy are kept alive.

166 | ANNE FRANK HOUSE
Otto made it his mission to share the lessons of the past with others.

176 | LEARN FROM THE PAST, LOOK TO THE FUTURE
Anne's legacy remains powerful, 75 years after her death.

186 | INDEX

Lessons From the Past

Laureen Nussbaum, a noted Holocaust scholar and a childhood friend of Anne, shares how she first came to learn of Anne's diary and the impact her words still have on us today.

ALTHOUGH IT DATES BACK 75 YEARS BY NOW, THE IMAGE OF Otto Frank, Anne's father, standing in my parents' living room remains etched into my memory. He was about to leave, his right hand stretched out for a goodbye handshake, a folder with Anne's writings wedged under his left arm. It must have been early in the fall of 1945, a few months after Otto's return from Auschwitz. He was one of the very few who had survived that place of horror and the only one of the eight people who were hidden in the Secret Annex to outlive Hitler's Third Reich.

It is well-known by now that, after the Secret Annex was raided on August 4, 1944, and its occupants rounded up, Otto's secretary, Miep Gies, and his stenographer, Bep Voskuijl, had sneaked up to the attic and gathered Anne's diaries and loose papers. Mrs. Gies, knowing how much these writings meant to Anne, had locked them away, hoping to return them to the young author after the war. Alas, Anne never came back, so her written legacy went to her father, who was deeply moved by what he read.

In May of 1944, Anne had started to rewrite her spontaneous diary entries, hoping to publish her revised text as an epistolary novel—i.e., a novel written in the form of letters. Otto wanted to fulfill his daughter's wish and so, after the war, he visited his few remaining Amsterdam friends, including my parents, to sound them out about the idea of publishing Anne's diary.

It is likely that everybody encouraged him, yet it was not easy to find a publisher. People in the business feared that the public would not be interested in the horrors of the recent past. Their readers were eager to catch up on what had been written outside occupied Europe and most of them wanted to look forward, not backward. But by June 1947, the Dutch publishing house Contact brought out the first edition of *Het Achterhuis* (*The Secret Annex*). Unfortunately, it did not reveal that Otto Frank had produced an amalgam of Anne's original diary entries and her much more sophisticated rewrites. In fact, it is not even mentioned that Otto Frank edited his daughter's writings.

Now, more than seven decades after *Het Achterhuis* was first published, it is amazing that there is still so much worldwide interest in Anne Frank, her book and the museum into which her hiding place has been converted. Why would that be? Jacob Boas, himself born in a concentration camp, and Alexandra Zapruder each published a book with translated excerpts of diaries, written during the Holocaust by Jewish teenagers all over occupied Europe. These texts are very authentic and heart-rending, but they have few readers.

Otto Frank (far left) served as best man at Laureen and Rudi Nussbaum's wedding in 1947.

Otto Frank originally published, was given a generous sampling of this more mature writing.

Still, why our fascination with *The Diary of Anne Frank*? It is a question each of us must answer for him- or herself. Does reading about horrible events far away in space and time give us some titillation mixed with a sense of relief that they are not happening here and now? Or does Anne's diary have a message for us?

I, for one, have always felt that Anne and other friends, as well as my relatives who suffered in the concentration camps, were calling out to me: "Make sure that this outrage will never happen again; see to it, that history does not repeat itself!" Then I look at the disastrous wars in Afghanistan and in the Middle East, at starvation in Africa, at unlivable conditions in Latin America and at what is happening at our own Southern border: families ripped apart, children in cages…and I feel downcast and ashamed. We were supposed to have learned our lessons and to do better and we have failed miserably!

Perhaps you want to delve into this new book about Anne Frank and her diary with a heightened awareness of the charge the Nazis' victims had for all of us: "Make sure that it will not happen again!" ∎

Laureen Nussbaum, PhD, is professor emerita in World Languages and Literatures at Portland State University in Oregon. Born in Frankfurt, Germany in 1927, her family and the Franks were friendly both there and in Amsterdam, and she continued her friendship with Otto Frank after the war. She, her husband and their three children moved to the U.S. in 1957; she is a noted Holocaust scholar and the author of Shedding Our Stars: The Story of Hans Calmeyer and How He Saved Thousands of Families Like Mine.

Yet for millions of people all over the world, it is Anne Frank's diary that has opened the gate to the alarming chapter of history that is rightly called the Holocaust, the annihilation of European Jewry.

There are at least three reasons why this would be the case. Foremost, *The Diary of Anne Frank* was the first one of this genre, and the Goodrich/Hackett play and subsequent George Stevens film based on it did their share to make "Anne Frank" a household name. Secondly, the fact that this name rolls so easily over everybody's tongue as compared to, say, Yitskhok Rudashevski, makes Anne Frank an ideal icon, with whom people can readily identify. Last but not least, Anne was a remarkably gifted writer, thoughtful in her use of words, with an ability for nuanced observation and a subtle sense of humor. This comes particularly through in her revised "literary" version, published in May 2019 as *Liebe Kitty* (*Dear Kitty*). Luckily, the average reader, who is only familiar with the book

CHAPTER 1

EARLY LIFE

Born into a loving, well-to-do family in 1929, Anne had a happy young childhood in Germany. Although her father experienced financial reverses in the early 1930s, those troubles were nothing compared to the dark days ahead.

Otto said Edith "was an excellent mother, who went to any lengths for her children."

"I Was Born Happy"

Anne's earliest years in Frankfurt were filled with love and joy, surrounded by friends and family in comfort. But storm clouds were forming on the horizon.

ANNELIES MARIE FRANK WAS STRONG-WILLED FROM THE moment she was born on the morning of June 12, 1929, in Frankfurt, Germany. Although she was a healthy 8½ pounds, she struggled to take her first few breaths. Her parents, Otto and Edith Frank, were relieved once the baby let out a good cry—which, much to their dismay, continued nonstop when she arrived home after 12 days in the hospital. "Has been screaming all night for the past six weeks," Edith noted in Anne's baby book. The days weren't much easier: The newborn was restless and uncomfortable due to the summer heat. Her exhausted parents took turns caring for her, and Otto often spent his night duty massaging Anne's upset belly.

The Franks' youngest daughter was quite the opposite of their elder child, Margot. Nicknamed "Little Angel," the 3-year-old hardly ever cried as a baby and grew to be a content toddler. And when her little sister arrived, there wasn't an ounce of jealousy. Margot was so enamored of Anne, a real-life version of her baby dolls, that she would jump

The Franks feared for their safety once their landlord at 307 Marbachweg became a Nazi sympathizer.

at the chance to change her diaper or take her for a walk. As Anne grew, so did her energetic spirit. The little girl with wild dark hair, protruding ears and a slight overbite (a trait she inherited from her father) easily charmed those around her with her infectious laugh. She was spoiled with love and attention, especially by Otto—whom she and Margot affectionately called "Pim."

Otto's wealth as the son of millionaires (his father owned the Michael Frank Bank, which Otto inherited after his father's death in 1909, and his mother, Alice Stern Frank, was from a well-to-do family) afforded his own family quite a luxurious life in those early years. "In his youth, Father led the life of a rich man's son," Anne later described in her diary on May 8, 1944. "Parties every week, balls, banquets, beautiful girls, waltzing, dinners,

a huge house, etc." In 1927, a year after Margot was born, Otto and Edith moved into a large home of two separate apartments connected by a staircase at 307 Marbachweg, located on the outskirts of Frankfurt. The Jewish Franks stood out in the middle-class neighborhood, but not because of their religion. While most men were teachers or government officials, Otto was a businessman who employed a live-in housekeeper for his wife. Despite the contrast, they lived in relative harmony with their diverse neighbors and grew particularly close to two Catholic families, the Stabs and the Naumanns.

"Those years on Marbachweg were among our best times," Edith fondly recalled in 1933, after financial setbacks forced the Franks to downsize to nearby Ganghoferstraße in 1931. The Wall Street

Left: Despite vastly different personalities, Margot and Anne were close. Bottom: Margot helps change baby Anne.

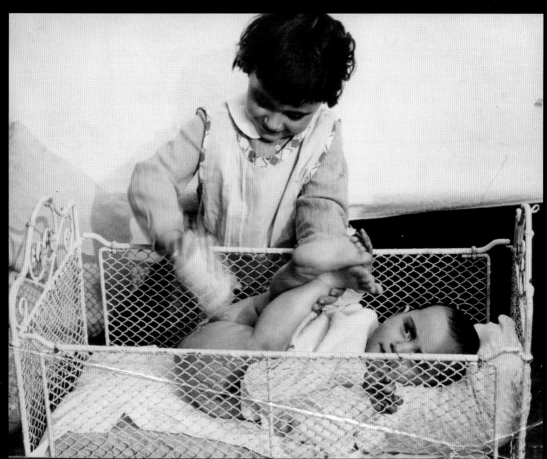

crash of 1929 had devastated Michael Frank Bank and business declined 90 percent over the next few years. Their woes worsened once Nazi leader Adolf Hitler came into power in January 1933 and issued a boycott on Jewish store owners, including doctors and lawyers. Otto feared it was just a matter of time before banks were added to the list of banned businesses and his faltering company would go bankrupt (Michael Frank Bank did finally dissolve in January 1934).

Between the dying economy and mass unemployment, the mood in Germany was growing increasingly dark—an unrest that was stoked by Hitler. Otto and Edith did all they could to distract their daughters from the evils brewing outside their door, even as it grew closer. Otto especially worried about how Hitler's hatred of Jews was affecting his children. That April, it was ruled Jewish educators who opposed Nazi beliefs would be fired, and Margot's principal and teacher at the private Ludwig Richter School were dismissed. Now prohibited from sending her to public school, the Franks transferred 7-year-old Margot (Anne was to enter kindergarten the following year) to Varrentrapp, where Jewish students were forced to sit in a corner segregated from their Christian classmates.

MEET THE FRANKS

OTTO

Born on May 12, 1889, the second son of millionaires Michael and Alice Frank forged his own path. After studying art history in college, Otto headed to New York City for traineeships at various banks and Macy's department store. Following his father's sudden death in 1909, he returned to Germany and enlisted in World War I, working up to lieutenant before he quit to join the family business, Michael Frank Bank. Otto found his one true love four days before his 36th birthday, and the longtime bachelor wed Edith Holländer, a decade his junior, following a whirlwind two-month courtship. The newlyweds settled in Frankfurt, where they lived with his mother for a year until they could afford their own place. As a father, Otto shined and was beloved for his warmth with his daughters (and their friends), earning him the nickname "Pim."

EDITH

Like Otto, the youngest daughter of Abraham and Rosa Holländer was born into a wealthy family, on January 16, 1900, and enjoyed a life of dinner parties, tennis games and holidays by the sea. Edith first met her future husband at a mutual friend's engagement party, but it wasn't until the two ran into each other while on vacation in San Remo, Italy, in 1925, that they fell in love (the city was so special to the couple, they returned for their honeymoon). Why the rush to marry? According to Anne, her father, who had been engaged once before, settled on Edith as "the best replacement for his fiancée." The two were opposite in many ways—she celebrated Jewish holidays and ate kosher foods, while he was not observant—and their parenting styles also differed. Edith was serious and strict compared to her outwardly loving husband.

As Hitler continued to isolate Jews in Germany, Otto knew the only way he could assuredly save his family was to flee the country. But where would they go? He considered Switzerland, where his sister Helene had been living. He also had extended family in Paris and London. Another option was the Netherlands, where he had opened a branch of the Michael Frank Bank a decade earlier after World War I, when Amsterdam became the European center for currency trading. Holland seemed like the Franks' best chance: Not only did Otto have a familiarity with the country and its language, but Jews made up 10 percent of the population in the capital, and the Dutch were accepting of the minority.

In August 1933, Edith and their daughters temporarily moved in with her mother, Rosa Holländer, and brothers Julius and Walter in Aachen, Germany, while Otto immigrated to Amsterdam to set up his new business and find his family a suitable home. "Because so many of my German countrymen were turning into hordes of nationalistic, cruel, anti-Semitic criminals, I had to draw conclusions," he later explained. "And though this did hurt me deeply, I realized that Germany was not the world, and I left my country forever." ∎

MARGOT

Otto and Edith wasted no time starting their family, welcoming their first child on February 16, 1926, just nine months after their wedding. The new parents gave their daughter Margot a middle name that honored her roots: Betti, after Edith's sister Bettina, who had died at a young age. An absolute delight to everyone, Margot was angelic, obedient, polite, bright (she excelled in every subject at school) and "a little princess," according to the Franks' live-in housekeeper Kathi Stilgenbauer. Close to her mother, Margot also inherited much of Edith's personality—which led to an intense two-against-one dynamic whenever she clashed with her spirited younger sister. "It's obvious that Mummy would stick up for Margot," Anne complained in her diary. "She and Margot always do back each other up."

ANNE

On June 12, 1929, the Franks' quiet household was turned upside down when their second daughter entered the world. A colicky infant who frazzled Otto and Edith during her first few months, Anne blossomed into quite the little chatterbox with a naughty side only Otto could control. To settle the adoring daddy's girl, he would entertain her with stories he would make up on the spot. Anne's favorite was "The Two Paulas," presumably about her and Margot: Good Paula never gave her parents any trouble, while Bad Paula often acted naughty. The characterization of the two sisters echoed how Anne once described herself and Margot: "She's naturally good, kind and clever, perfection itself, but I seem to have enough mischief for the two of us."

WHY DID HITLER HATE THE JEWS SO MUCH?

Ever since the end of World War I in 1918, Adolf Hitler held an intense resentment toward the Jews: He believed they played a role in Germany's defeat, which resulted in the country plunging into chaos and famine. And he was dedicated to getting revenge.

"Once I really am in power, my first and foremost task will be the annihilation of the Jews," vowed Hitler, a soldier who was wounded in the war. "As soon as I have the power to do so, I will have gallows built in rows.... Then the Jews will be hanged indiscriminately, and they will remain hanging until they stink; they will hang there as long as the principles of hygiene permit. As soon as they have been untied, the next batch will be strung up, and so on down the line, until the last Jew in Munich has been exterminated. Other cities will follow suit, precisely in this fashion, until all Germany has been completely cleansed of Jews."

After Hitler was discharged from the army in 1920, he joined the far-right National Socialist German Workers Party, also known as the Nazis, quickly earning a reputation for his vitriolic speeches—and ultimately becoming the party's chairman. While in prison for a failed coup, he outlined his plans in the 1925 manifesto *Mein Kampf* (*My Struggle*): the long-overdue extermination of Jews, "the personification of the devil as the symbol of all evil."

Over the following years, as the Nazis steadily grew more powerful, Hitler relentlessly pushed his propaganda: All of the country's problems were because of what the Jews had done a decade earlier. In the 1930 election, the party leveraged the economic disaster—the fault of Jewish financiers, they claimed—to earn 6.4 million votes, raising the number of Nazi representatives in the Reichstag, Germany's parliament, from 12 to 107 and becoming the second-largest party after the Social Democrats. Over the next two years, the economy continued to tumble as Nazi support was on the rise, and by 1932, the party doubled its number of Reichstag seats.

In January 1933, Hitler finally reached the necessary level to put his plan into action: He was named chancellor of Germany. With the passing of the Enabling Act, he assumed absolute power to rule the country as a dictator —and he got right to work. In March, the first Nazi-managed concentration camp was established at Dachau. On April 1, at precisely 10 a.m., Hitler implemented a nationwide boycott of Jewish-owned businesses. That was followed by bans on "non-Aryan" lawyers, dentists, armed forces employees, government civil servants and journalists. Just as he hoped, Jewish unemployment skyrocketed across Germany.

But this was only just the beginning of his plans. "We are going to destroy the Jews," Hitler vowed. "They are not going to get away with what they did on November 9, 1918. The day of reckoning has come."

Hitler was portrayed as Germany's savior and blamed the Jews for its economic disaster.

Anne spent her early years surrounded by loving family and friends

Maart 1927 Frankfort

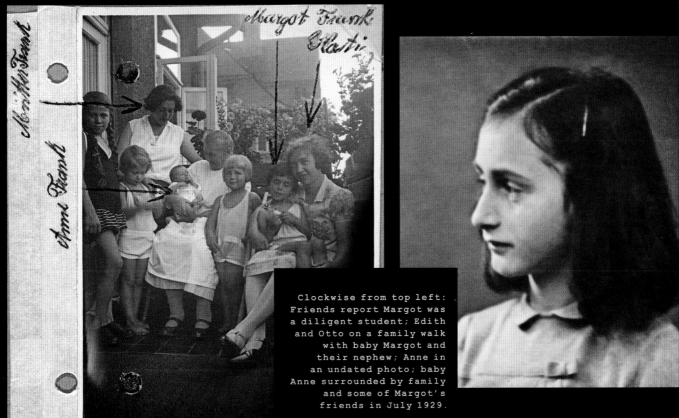

Margot Frank
Blati

Mother Frank

Anne Frank

Clockwise from top left: Friends report Margot was a diligent student; Edith and Otto on a family walk with baby Margot and their nephew; Anne in an undated photo; baby Anne surrounded by family and some of Margot's friends in July 1929.

HERINNERING
AAN MIJN
SCHOOLJAAR
1935

Clockwise from top left:
Anne dressed for a
school day; infant Anne
sleeping in her crib;
playing in a sandbox
under her mother's
watchful eye in 1931;
in class at the 6th
Montessori School
in Amsterdam.

"I KNOW HOW
SAD YOU WERE
BECAUSE WE ALL
LEFT GERMANY,
BUT I HOPE YOUR
AFFECTION FOR
OUR FAMILY
WILL NOT FADE."
Alice Stern Frank to
neighbor Gertrud Naumann

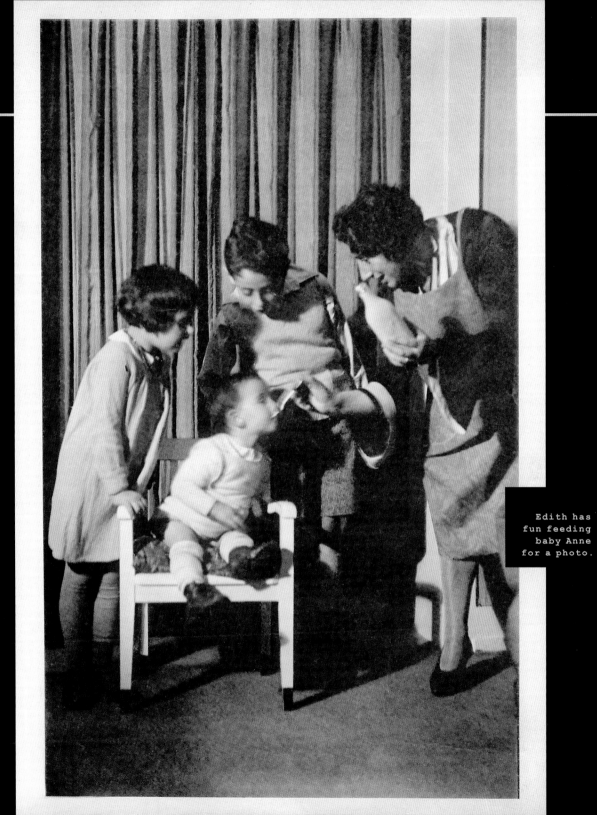

Edith has
fun feeding
baby Anne
for a photo.

Clockwise from top:
Edith Holländer and
Otto Frank on their
wedding day in 1925;
Anne in an undated
photo; on a boat ride;
Anne in 1937.

des neue Roffer

Clockwise from
top left: Margot
and her maternal
grandmother in
1929; Anne in a
new coat in 1941;
Margot cycling
in Amsterdam
in 1939.

CHAPTER 2

NAZI THREAT

After fleeing anti-Semitism in Germany, the Franks settled in Amsterdam. For a while, Margot and Anne enjoyed a typical Dutch childhood. But it soon became clear that the family hadn't escaped Hitler's reach.

Hitler
drew large
crowds at his
appearances,
like this
rally in
Nuremberg
in 1933.

RUNNING FROM
HITLER

As the Nazi leader grew more powerful, the Frank family fled Germany for Holland—but the dictator's evil empire followed them.

SEPT. 11 1934
Jhr ↓ Gewicht

kg 24 25 2 kg

PHOTOWAA
BAD AAC

A photo-booth portrait from September 1934 displays Anne's weight (approximately 54 pounds).

ONCE ADOLF HITLER ASSUMED ABSOLUTE POWER IN 1933, an estimated 37,000 German Jews had the same idea as the Franks to flee the country immediately. During this wave of emigration, refugees settled throughout Western Europe in the Netherlands, France, Belgium, Denmark and Switzerland, all hoping for a fresh start away from the constant threat of persecution. As for the Franks, they relocated to a newly constructed development in Amsterdam's River Quarter called Merwedeplein, a triangle-shaped cluster of modern housing buildings that extended out from a 12-story high-rise and surrounded a large courtyard, "The Merry," tailor-made for adventurous children like Anne Frank. And there were plenty of familiar faces for her to play with: The predominantly Jewish area was also home to a number of German exiles, including Joseph and Marianne Klein and their three young daughters, whom the Franks knew from Frankfurt.

While the reminders of their German roots were comforting, life was certainly different in Amsterdam. The Franks' second-floor apartment paled in comparison to their two-story duplex back on Marbachweg—and was even smaller than their downsized home in Ganghoferstraße. "There is no room in our bedroom for anything except the beds," Edith complained. "No cellar, no pantry, but everything is bright, convenient and warm." And for the first two months, their home was also quiet, as Anne remained in Aachen, Germany, with her maternal grandmother while Otto and Edith prepared Margot to start school. The family finally reunited on February 16, 1934, when their elder daughter awoke on her eighth birthday to a special gift: Her little sister dressed in a white tutu sitting on the kitchen table.

As they settled into their new surroundings, "Anne has made the adjustment better than Margot," Edith reported to a former neighbor back in Frankfurt. The 4-year-old made friends in the neighborhood as easily as she picked up Dutch. And once she started kindergarten that May, she became even more popular. On her very first day at the Montessori school, where many of the students

"OUR LIVES WERE NOT WITHOUT ANXIETY, SINCE OUR RELATIVES IN GERMANY WERE SUFFERING UNDER HITLER'S ANTI-JEWISH LAWS."
Anne Frank

After weeks of uprising in the Warsaw Ghetto, Polish Jews were captured and deported in 1943.

were German Jews, Anne met a girl much like herself: Hanneli "Lies" Goslar, who was also new to Amsterdam and only spoke German. "I didn't know the language yet and my mother was very apprehensive about how it would go, how I would react," recounted Hanneli. "But I came in and Anne was standing across from the door at the little bells and was ringing them. She turned and I threw myself into her arms and my mother went home feeling confident. I had abandoned my shyness and at the same time forgotten all about my mother."

Despite their common bond, the girls were actually quite different: Anne was a chatterbox with a mischievous side, while Hanneli was shy

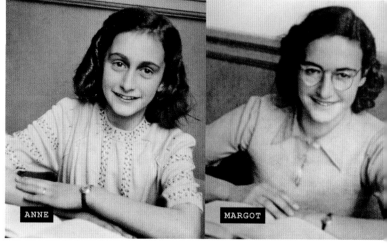

ANNE

MARGOT

NOT THE ONLY VICTIMS

Although Jews are the group most associated with the Holocaust, there were many more "subhumans" targeted by Adolf Hitler's hatred. During his reign of power in the 1930s and 1940s, the Nazi leader also persecuted and murdered at least 3 million Soviet POWs, 1.8 million ethnic Poles, 200,000 physically and mentally disabled people, 90,000 Roma (Gypsies), 50,000 homosexuals and thousands of Jehovah's Witnesses. "Those who will not change their ways will be bent and broken," Hitler proclaimed. "Capital punishment for betrayers of their country and people."

The majority of these people died in concentration camps, where they were sentenced to forced labor for their arbitrary "crimes"—but scores more were killed in mass shootings, public massacres called "pogroms," and death marches. When Germany invaded Poland in 1939, the purpose was to exterminate 85 percent of the population and turn the remaining 15 percent into slaves. Within three months, 60,000 innocent people were executed. Similarly, Nazis invaded the Soviet Union in June 1941, with the goal of repopulating it with Germans and using captured civilians as slaves.

and reserved. Once the two linked up with Susanne "Sanne" Ledermann—who, like Hanneli, was more subdued and serious—the trio of best friends was inseparable. "People who saw us together used to say, 'There goes Anne, Hanne and Sanne,'" Anne later boasted in her diary.

Outside of school, the girls spent their days playing hide-and-seek and hopscotch, roller-skating, shooting marbles, perfecting cartwheels and jumping rope with many of the other kids in "The Merry." "In the winter, if there was snow on the ground, Anne pulled me around our horseshoe-shaped street on a small wooden sled," described Juliane Duke. "I remember hanging on and both of us laughing when we went over a bump." Over the next five years, 16,000 exiled Jews sought refuge in the River Quarter, so Anne always had plenty of friends around to keep her company.

But it wasn't all fun and games. At school, the Montessori curriculum allowed each student to start the day studying whatever they desired, and for Anne, that was reading—but she didn't pick it up as easily as Margot, one of the top students in her class. In a letter to family in January 1935, Edith wrote, "Anne is learning to read with great difficulty," and she underlined "with great difficulty" for emphasis. One thing Anne did excel at was talking in class, and she often had to stay behind at school after the bell rang as punishment. Friends may have found Anne's inability to remain quiet amusing, but it was "troublesome" to her father. "She would constantly ask questions, not just when we were alone, but also when others were present," he revealed. "If we had visitors, it was rather difficult to get rid of her, because she was interested in everything and everyone.... It was good that Anne could attend a Montessori school, where all pupils were treated as individuals."

Inside the Frank home, it was a similar situation: All of their daughters' friends were welcome, no matter their religion or homeland—and they all got to enjoy the family's German delicacies. Edith would often treat their little guests to rolls topped with cream cheese and chocolate, with

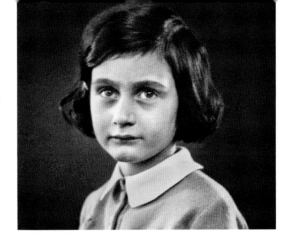

Anne, at age 8 (top) and age 10 (middle) was known as a chatterbox at her Montessori school in 1936.

"AFTER THE EXPERIENCES IN NAZI GERMANY, WE COULD LIVE OUR OWN LIFE IN THE NETHERLANDS."

Otto Frank

Anne posed with her friend Isa's dog Dopy in 1940.

homemade lemonade and bottled milk to drink. As for Otto, he'd entertain them with jokes, as well as games and stories he'd make up on a whim. "My first impression of Otto was of his kindness," remembers Eva Schloss, whose family lived on the same block as the Franks after emigrating from Austria. "After a few preemptive discussions at the Franks' apartment, Otto realized that I still spoke little Dutch. From then on he went out of his way to form a bond with me and make me feel at home by speaking German. I knew him for many years and, despite all that we went through, I never changed my opinion that he was warm and empathetic— a true gentleman." Otto was just as hospitable to the parents of his daughters' friends. During the Klein family's early days in Amsterdam, "[He] advised my father [Joseph Klein] as to how to set up a wholesale business in clothing accessories and notions such as buttons, belts and buckles," according to Laureen Nussbaum (who was then known as Hannelore Klein).

While Otto's advice to Joseph Klein proved fruitful, he was spinning his wheels when it came to his own business. The former bank owner was putting in endless hours as a traveling salesman for Opekta, his brother-in-law Erich Elias' company that sold spices and pectin (a setting agent for making jam)—but with little monetary return. Oftentimes, Otto later revealed, he could barely "put food on the table," and the stress took its toll. "Mr. Frank hasn't taken any time off and looks thin and tired," Edith wrote in an October 1934 letter. "Business prospects are unfortunately very poor, but we mustn't lose heart." As Opekta limped along, the Franks rented out a large room on the second floor of their apartment to make ends meet.

Otto and Edith succeeded in distracting their daughters from the family's struggles, but they couldn't shield them from what was percolating outside their home. Back in Nazi Germany, life was growing increasingly bleak for Jews—and as thousands of exiles poured into the Netherlands, the Dutch were becoming less tolerant of outsiders. "Each day, more and more refugees from Germany

In their last known family photo, Margot, Otto, Anne and Edith pose in an Amsterdam neighborhood in 1941.

DADDY'S GIRL & MOMMY'S GIRL

Anne and Margot may have had complete opposite personalities, but one could say they found perfect matches in their parents: The younger girl was especially close with the outwardly loving Otto, and her older sister tended to act more like the introverted, reserved Edith. "Margot seemed to be Mommy's little girl," noted family friend Miep Gies, "and Anne was very much Daddy's."

Otto and Edith expressed their love in vastly different ways: "The most adorable father I've ever seen," according to Anne, was equally warm and affectionate with both of his daughters (as well as to their friends when they would come by), while her mother was less demonstrative. It was a trait Margot inherited, and it sometimes created an intense two-against-one dynamic in the home whenever the sisters clashed.

Anne so adored her father, "the only one who understands me," that whenever she had to share his attention with her sister, it was crushing. "If he holds Margot up as an example, approves of what she does, praises and caresses her, then something gnaws at me inside," she admitted. "He is the one I look up to. I don't love anyone in the world but him."

AMERICAN PEN PALS

As fears grew in the Netherlands, the Frank girls had an outlet in a pair of sisters on the other side of the world. In 1940, a middle school teacher in Danville, Iowa, organized a pen pal exchange between her students and Anne's Montessori school in Amsterdam. That April, Anne received a letter from 10-year-old Juanita Wagner, who detailed living on a farm with her mother and older sister, Betty Ann. In Anne's reply, she talked about her school, postcard collection (she even included one featuring Amsterdam scenery for Juanita) and her upcoming 11th birthday.

Anne and Juanita's sisters also got to communicate, although Margot's letter to Betty Ann was far less lighthearted: The 14-year-old opened up about her worries, especially with the Nazi threat. "We often listen to the radio, for these are stressful times," Margot wrote in English (Otto translated for his daughters to hand-copy). "We never feel safe, because we border directly on Germany and we are only a small country."

In Anne's note to Juanita, she ended with a special request: "In case you and Betty get a photo do send a copy as I am curious to know how you look." The Wagner sisters complied, but their response never reached Anne and Margot: By then, the Netherlands had been invaded and was under the control of Germany.

Throughout World War II, Juanita and Betty Ann often wondered about the Frank sisters. Once it was over, they wrote again to the Merwedeplein address. This time, they received a response from Mr. Frank, who delivered the heartbreaking news that their pen pals had not survived. In 1988, Anne and Margot's letters to the Wagners were auctioned for $165,000, purchased by an anonymous bidder who donated them to the Simon Wiesenthal Center in Los Angeles.

Amsterdam.
Nieuwe Brug over de Amstel,

Anne told her pen pal that she collected postcards, like this vintage one of Amsterdam.

were moving into our neighborhood, mostly Jews," explained Miep Gies, who worked at Opekta, "and the joke became that on the No. 8 streetcar 'the ticket-taker also speaks Dutch.' Many of these refugees were more affluent than the Dutch workers in the neighborhood, and they created a stir when seen in furs or with other fancy possessions." To not draw attention to their roots in public, Otto instructed Margot and Anne to only speak Dutch, even though at home they conversed in Dutch and German.

By early 1939, as the Nazis ramped up their removal of Jews in Germany, it was feared they would next come for Dutch Jews. Instead, on September 1, Hitler invaded Poland, rounded up the estimated 3.5 million Jews and imprisoned them in ghettos while he prepared their final destination, one of the hundreds of death camps Nazis were establishing across the country.

Eight months later, May 10, 1940, turned out to be the day the Dutch were dreading. As German troops advanced into the Netherlands, Queen Wilhelmina came on the radio urging her people to remain calm. Still, panic set in: Telephone service was interrupted, air-raid alarms continually sounded and people rushed to grocery stores to stock up on nonperishable food. Although Amsterdam was not yet occupied, as a precaution, the Franks kept Margot and Anne home from school. Over the following days, as the hysteria spread, many Jews scrambled to leave the Netherlands—only to be stopped at checkpoints and turned away. Others took drastic measures and committed suicide rather than wait to be rounded up and taken away by Nazis. The Franks remained in Amsterdam, and on May 15, the Netherlands surrendered.

Under Germany's rule, Hitler appointed Arthur Seyss-Inquart as Reich commissioner. In his inauguration speech on May 29, he echoed Hitler's claims that the occupation was more of a protection: "We Germans have not come to subjugate this country and its people, nor do we seek to impose our political system on them." But that promise didn't apply to the Jewish population, as they soon found out. "After May 1940, the good times were few and far between," Anne later wrote in her diary. "The arrival of the Germans is when the trouble started for the Jews." ■

Nazis Arrive in Amsterdam

By 1940, Germany had invaded the Netherlands, with a special focus on the capital city's Jewish population.

BEFORE THE START OF WORLD WAR II, AN ESTIMATED 154,000 Jews were living in the Netherlands, a safe distance from Nazi Germany. But once Adolf Hitler invaded Poland on September 1, 1939, it was growing more difficult—and dangerous—for the Dutch to remain neutral, as they had in World War I. This time around, Germany intended to occupy the Netherlands (as well as Belgium and Luxembourg) as part of a larger effort to eventually conquer France. But due to bad weather throughout the winter months, Hitler's plans were postponed several times, until that spring.

At dawn on May 10, 1940, German aircraft were seen flying over the Netherlands, but it was assumed they were heading to England. After reaching the North Sea, the planes turned around—bound for their respective targets. In the South Holland province, paratroopers descended on the shores of Rotterdam. About a dozen miles away, in The Hague, Germans bombed military airfields in an effort to capture the government. By the time they made their way to the eastern side of the country, Dutch soldiers were waiting, but their outdated weaponry (from World War I) only succeeded in slowing the invaders as they advanced into the Netherlands.

After four long days of battle, Germany delivered an ultimatum on May 14: Surrender that afternoon or Rotterdam would be bombed. But before the deadline even approached, planes descended on the city's downtown area. When the attack was finally over, 850 innocent civilians were killed and 80,000 more left homeless—but the Nazis weren't done. They threatened to bomb the province of Utrecht next, and so on, unless the country surrendered. The Dutch had no other option but to agree, and on May 15, the Netherlands conceded and became a German-occupied territory.

That same day, Nazi soldiers drove into Amsterdam—and to the horror of Dutch Jews, were warmly welcomed by the locals. As they crossed the city's Berlage Bridge, throngs of people enthusiastically gave them the Nazi salute. At city hall, the Germans were provided with a map of Amsterdam. Upon their arrival in the village of Duivendrecht, Amsterdam Deputy Mayor Kropman greeted Gen. Carl von Tiedemann with a handshake. In return, he was assured the Jewish population would be left in peace. "If the Jews don't want to see us," von Tiedemann offered, "we don't see the Jews." But they would soon learn that his words were meaningless. ∎

In Nuremberg, Germany, in 1934, Hitler greeted his followers with his very own salute.

The Nazis often relied on forced labor among the populations they occupied, including Poland and the Netherlands.

No Jews Allowed

Under the German occupation, Adolf Hitler imposed tight restrictions on Dutch Jews—with the ultimate goal of excluding them from society altogether.

ONCE GERMANY INVADED AND OCCUPIED THE NETHERLANDS, life changed dramatically for Dutch Jews—but it didn't happen overnight. Five months later, "our freedom was severely restricted," Anne recalled, as Adolf Hitler systematically rolled out a series of anti-Jewish decrees intended to marginalize them. In October 1940, it began with prohibiting ritual slaughter, a vital aspect of Jewish dietary laws that deem food as kosher (fit to eat). Throughout the rest of the year, Jews were removed from government employment (including teachers) and banned from recreational facilities, hotels, restaurants, parks and beaches. They were also forbidden to use public transportation or ride in cars (even their own), and were only allowed to do their shopping between 3 and 5 p.m. And that was just the beginning.

In January 1941, all Jews in the country were ordered to register. With the help of Dutch officials, 160,820 people, including the Franks, were recorded for the Nazis. Soon after, every Dutch person over age 15 was required to carry an identity card—those belonging to Jews were stamped with a large recognizable "J." "We do not consider the Jews to be members of the Dutch nation," explained Arthur Seyss-Inquart, the Austrian Nazi in command of the Netherlands, in a speech that March. "To us, the Jews are not Dutch. The Jews are the enemy with whom no armistice or peace can be made. Do not expect me to lay this down in a regulation except in police measures. We will smite the Jews where we meet them and whoever goes along with them must take the consequences."

Since the start of the occupation, many Jewish shops, cafés and monuments were destroyed by the WA (short for Weerbaarheidsafdeling, the Nazi assault group) with the help of other anti-Semites. On February 9, 1941, they targeted Amsterdam's Café Alcazar, resulting in the death of one WA member. As punishment, German police organized a raid on Jonas Daniël Meijerplein square—just 3 miles from Anne's home—where they rounded up 427 random Jewish men between 18 and 35 and deported them to the Mauthausen concentration

Jews in Warsaw, Poland, surrendered to the Nazis in 1943, after Hitler warned, "Europe cannot find peace until the Jewish question has been solved."

"THERE WAS A TIME WHEN THE JEWS IN GERMANY ALSO LAUGHED AT MY PROPHECIES.... TAKE MY WORD FOR IT: THEY WILL STOP LAUGHING EVERYWHERE."

Adolf Hitler, September 1942

camp in Austria. (All but one died.) The non-Jews of Amsterdam were so alarmed by the brutality that they staged a two-day protest with more than 300,000 people taking part and brought the city to a halt—but they were met with more violence from the Nazis: Some strikers were shot, and many more arrested. The city of Amsterdam itself was heavily fined and the mayor was ousted. That June, another raid arrested 300 Jewish men in their homes and on the streets. They too were sent to Mauthausen and their families were later informed they were "dead" or had been "shot on the run."

Anne was especially upset about the turbulence that came with the German occupation. What would it mean for her family? She would often have nightmares and run crying into her mother and father's bedroom for comfort. "Sleeping with Daddy is very nice," she wrote to her paternal grandmother, Alice Stern Frank, "but I wish that there was another reason that I could sleep downstairs and that the times were normal again."

But it only got worse for the young girl when the regulation came down on August 8, 1941: Jewish children must attend separate schools. That meant the seventh-grader would have to transfer from her beloved Montessori, which she had attended since kindergarten. Saying goodbye to her principal, Mrs. Hendrika Kuperus, was especially hard: "At the end of the year, we were both in tears as we said a heartbreaking farewell," recalled Anne.

By 1942, the restrictions became tighter—and more concerning. In April, all Jews were required to deposit their money into designated German-controlled banks and had to surrender most of their other valuables, such as jewelry, gold, art and antiques, which were sold (the money was used to pay for the deportation of Jews via train, as well as the expansion of Westerbork transit camp, where they were held before being sent to concentration camps).

On May 3, Nazis introduced yellow Star of David badges that all Jews age 6 and older had to wear to make them easily identifiable. To add insult to injury, they were made to purchase four badges each, at four cents apiece. Anyone not wearing their yellow star would be severely punished, possibly even sentenced to a concentration camp. In June, Jews were given a mandatory curfew: They could not be out on the streets between 8 p.m. and 6 a.m. That same month, Jews were required to turn in their bicycles—in perfect condition and including spare tires—within 48 hours. But the Franks ignored this rule. They gave Edith's bicycle to Christian friends for safekeeping and hid Margot's inside their home in case of an emergency.

By late June, the situation for Jews was becoming dire—they just didn't know it yet. In a secret phone conversation between Nazi Lieutenant Colonel Adolf Eichmann and Nazi official Franz Rademacher, it was decided that 40,000 Jews from the Netherlands, as well as 50,000 more from German-occupied France and Belgium, were to be deported and sent to Auschwitz concentration camp in Poland for "labor service." When the Jewish Council was instructed to report how many people they'd be able to "assemble" and send on daily transport trains, they replied with 350 to 375. But that wasn't sufficient. The Nazis insisted they increase the number to 600 per day, every day. It was then declared that beginning on July 5, anyone who received a summons for labor service must report to the Jewish Council immediately. "Things are getting worse from day to day, as you probably know," Otto wrote to his family the day before, on July 4. "But don't worry, even if you don't hear much from us." ∎

THE FRANKS'
AMERICAN DREAMS

As Dutch Jews were threatened with deportation to concentration camps, the Franks once again found themselves desperate to flee the Nazis—and leave Europe altogether. Back in 1909, as a young man fresh out of college, Otto spent a year interning at Macy's in New York City and befriended Nathan Straus Jr., whose family owned the department store (pictured below). Over the three decades since, the two had remained close, and now Otto was relying on that bond to save his wife and children. On April 30, 1941, he wrote to Straus about acquiring visas for himself, Edith, Margot, Anne and his mother-in-law, Rosa Holländer. "It is for the sake of the children mainly that we have to care for. I would not ask if conditions here would not force me to do all I can in time to be able to avoid worse."

Straus—a former New York state senator who counted the Roosevelts among his friends—was willing to get involved, but he wanted to go through the proper channels. Along with his wife, Helen, he appealed to the State Department and the Migration Department at the National Refugee Service and vouched that Otto was "an extraordinarily fine man." On June 11, Straus signed five affidavits agreeing to sponsor the Franks, but it wouldn't be that easy. At the time, more than 300,000 names were on the waiting list to receive an immigration visa, forcing American consulates to tighten protocol: Visas wouldn't be granted unless transportation to the U.S. had been booked. Unfortunately for the Franks, by June 1941, most U.S. ambassadors in German-occupied areas had been expelled by the Nazis.

"Unless you can get to a place where there is an American Consul," Straus wrote to Otto on July 1, "there does not seem to be any way of arranging for you to come over." That same month, a new division took over visa prescreening, which meant new affidavits needed to be filled out on behalf of potential immigrants. The Franks were now back at square one—and time was running out.

Otto came up with a plan B: He would obtain a tourist visa to Cuba for himself, since each cost $2,000 (nearly $35,000 today), and then he would work to bring over his wife and children. By December, Edith's brothers Julius and Walter Holländer, who had immigrated to Boston, had prepared the money, but it was just too late: On December 11, following Japan's surprise attack on Pearl Harbor and Germany's declaration of war against the United States, the Cuban government canceled Otto's application. The Franks were trapped in Nazi-occupied Amsterdam with no way out.

CRUEL SUMMER

Despite the dark cloud of the German occupation in the Netherlands, for the first year, young Dutch Jews were not yet directly affected by Adolf Hitler's bans. That all changed in the spring of 1941, when they were forbidden from mixing with their non-Jewish classmates—soon followed by the rule they could only attend all-Jewish schools and be taught by Jewish teachers. "Anne and Margot Frank had been crazy about their school," said family friend Miep Gies. "I knew that both of them would be heartbroken." For Anne, leaving the beloved Montessori she had known since kindergarten was devastating.

That fall, Anne and Margot would be enrolled at the Jewish Lyceum—but until then, they were intent on making the most of their summer break. Unfortunately for the younger sister, that wouldn't include working on her tan: In May, Jews were banned from public beaches, swimming pools and parks. "We're not likely to get sunburned, because we can't go to the swimming pool," Anne complained in a letter to her paternal grandmother, Alice Frank—her "Omi"—in Switzerland. "Too bad, but there's nothing to be done." After celebrating her 12th birthday in June, she kicked off her summer with the wedding of Miep Santrouschitz and Jan Gies in Amsterdam before going out of town with Sanne Ledermann and her family to Beekbergen, about 50 miles away.

But for a lively girl like Anne, the trip was not nearly as exciting as she had hoped. "It's very nice here, but it's a pity the weather is so bad," she reported to her Omi on July 31. "The house is very old-fashioned but still pleasant." Cooped up inside, the girls passed much of their time reading, but before long, Anne had burned through every book she brought, as well as Sanne's. Bored and homesick, she wrote separate letters to her parents. Edith wasn't always prompt with her replies, which disappointed her daughter. "I haven't gotten a letter from Mother since Tuesday evening, and now it's Monday evening," Anne fussed to Otto. To appease her, the Franks sent care packages containing spending money (which she used on stamps, postcards, candy and a notebook), snacks and movie-star trading cards.

Back in Amsterdam, 15-year-old Margot was spending her days enjoying her favorite sport, rowing, as a member of the Society for the Promotion of Water Sports Among Young People. One highlight was the day her club made it to Frog Island, about 6 miles away. Margot's love of rowing was captured on film: In February 2020, in celebration of what would have been her 94th birthday, the Anne Frank House released two newly discovered photos of the teen with her team. In one, she's sitting in a boat; the other, laughing with a friend on the grass. "Margot was a beautiful, bright and sporty girl," says Teresien da Silva, head of collections at the Anne Frank House (which also has a first-place medal on display that Margot won for style rowing in 1940). "We already had some pictures of Margot on skis, on ice skates and on the tennis court, and now we also have photos of Margot with her rowing club. These new photos show a cheerful girl, enjoying herself with her crewmates."

That summer ended up being Margot's last with her cherished club. In September, Jews were banned from partaking in public sports, which meant she was no longer allowed to row or participate in matches (similarly, her Jewish coach Roos van Gelder was also relieved of her position). In an act of solidarity, Margot's non-Jewish teammates quit the team. "We had won several years in a row," friend Bella van der Wilk-Kohlweij said in 2011. "We trained often. When we heard that Margot could not row anymore, and that Roos van Gelder was not allowed to train us any longer, we were so angry that we decided unanimously to go on strike."

Upon her return from vacation with Sanne's family, Anne spent the remainder of her summer break playing with friends in the neighborhood and, on the weekends, accompanying her father to work at Opekta, where he taught her how to cook up jam. Once, when Otto had been called away in the middle of making a batch, Anne finished the job herself, which impressed managing director Johannes Kleiman. "Her whole manner said:

In this newly discovered photo, Margot (center in closest boat) posed with her crewmates near Berlage Bridge in 1941.

'I can handle this.' [Anne] was really interested and eager to learn. She wanted to know how to do things herself." Occasionally, Anne's friend Hanneli Goslar also tagged along, and the two would entertain themselves by playing with the typewriters and rubber stamps in the offices and using the telephones..

When summer came to a close, so did the fun and games. That September, Anne and Margot started school at the Jewish Lyceum, and it was a major adjustment for both girls. On the first day, "I was given the desk at the very back of the class, behind girls much bigger than myself," lamented Anne, who didn't know any of the students (Hanneli, who went by Lies, attended the same school, but was in a different class). "I felt lonely and forsaken. In the second hour I raised my hand and asked to be moved to another spot, as I could see very little unless I fairly hung into the aisle. The third hour was gym, and the teacher seemed so nice that I asked her to try to have Lies transferred to my room. How the dear lady did it I will never know, but the next hour, in walked Lies and was given the desk beside mine."

As for Margot, who had spent years at the elite Lyceum for Girls, sharing a class with male students was a new experience. At the start of the school year, she was one of four girls, strongly outnumbered by the 20 boys. But eventually, the teen grew to be interested in the male gaze. "Margot has plenty of company and is becoming livelier," Otto revealed to his mother. "She's paying more attention to her clothes and hairdo now." In a follow-up letter, her elder granddaughter reported an update: She and her new best friend Jetteke Frijda "ran around with the boys a lot" at first, however, "now we're not and it's a good thing, because they're getting too fresh."

Although Margot insisted she was happy at her new school, she still longed for the old days, before the German occupation and the endless restrictions that came with it. On several occasions, Margot was spotted by former classmate Hetty Last waiting with her bicycle outside the Lyceum for Girls as the students were dismissed for the day: "I think she really missed her old school and her non-Jewish friends." Hetty ventured

As Friends Knew Her

Jacqueline Van Maarsen,
Laureen Nussbaum,
Hanneli Goslar and
Eva Schloss share their
fondest memories of Anne
from their childhood
in their diverse
Dutch neighborhood.

WHILE THE WORLD WAS AN UNCERTAIN PLACE FOR JEWS during World War II, at "The Merry," all fears could dissipate for an afternoon over a game of marbles or a cartwheel challenge. The triangular courtyard at the Merwedeplein, the housing area that Anne Frank called home for eight years, was the epicenter of fun—and the place where many of her friends first met the vivacious girl with wild hair and a spirit to match. The Franks were one of the early families to move into the middle-class neighborhood, back when "The Merry" was still under construction and nothing more than a glorified sandbox, so Anne often acted as the welcoming committee for the younger residents.

Eva Schloss (née Geiringer) was a shy kid who spoke very little Dutch when Anne approached her shortly after she and her family moved from

JACQUELINE VAN MAARSEN

Anne loved to roll hoops and race scooters with her friends.

Belgium to 46 Merwedeplein, across the square from the Franks, in February 1940. "The apartments were small, and all the children played outside," Eva recalled 80 years later, in January 2020. "One day a little girl introduced herself to me; she was Anne Frank, we were both 11. I was still a tomboy and Anne was a real girl, interested in hairstyles and boys."

Eva got a glimpse at Anne's flair one day when she accompanied her mother to a local dressmaker to get a coat altered and overheard a shopper analyzing her outfit with a shop assistant: What did she think of the length of the hem? Would it look more stylish with big shoulder pads? "To my amazement the curtain was pulled back and there was Anne, swishing her new peach outfit with green trim as she surveyed herself in the mirror, contemplating the latest fashion trends from Paris."

When the Franks moved to the neighborhood in December 1933, they were only one of dozens of German-Jewish families, which soon included the Kleins, with whom they had been acquainted back in Frankfurt. Joseph and Marianne's three daughters were roughly the same ages as Margot and Anne, and the five girls often found adventure together in their new surroundings. "All of us youngsters relished our newfound freedom in the Netherlands, where we could ride our bikes and go anywhere without bumping into restrictions placed on Jews," middle daughter Hannelore Klein, who now goes by Laureen Nussbaum, writes in her 2019 Holocaust memoir *Shedding Our Stars*.

But as the girls got older, naturally the Kleins and Franks paired off into separate friend groups. Laureen—two years older than Anne, and a year-and-a-half younger than Margot—was right smack in between, but she often found herself drawn to the elder, "dignified" Frank sister, whom she viewed as a role model, rather than the "little talkative girl." Every Wednesday, Laureen and her older sister Susi would bike with Margot to their Jewish classes, "where we read the stories of the Old Testament and learned the Hebrew alphabet so we could follow the prayers and blessings during services." Although Anne was too young to attend, she and Laureen's younger sister Marli "came to the children's celebrations of some of the Jewish holidays."

At school, Anne acted no differently than she did on the playground. Hanneli "Lies" Goslar remembers her best friend since kindergarten as "a mischievous little girl" who got a kick out of taking her shoulder out of its socket, a trick that also got her excused from gym class. "She thought that it was great fun to have the other children watch and burst out laughing," Hanneli once told a Dutch documentary filmmaker. Although Eva did not attend the same school as Anne, she still heard all about her neighbor's antics. "She was actually a big chatterbox," Eva revealed during a lecture in Oceanside, New York, in November 2018. "Her nickname was 'Mrs. Quack, Quack.' She had to stay behind at school very often to write 100 times, 'I'm not going to talk so much in school.'"

It was a lesson Anne couldn't quite learn. When she and Hanneli transferred to the Jewish Lyceum

LAUREEN NUSSBAUM

ALL EYES ON ANNE

Whether she was gossiping with her girlfriends at a café or giving a class presentation, Anne loved having everybody's eyes on her. Laureen Nussbaum would often see Margot's younger sister on the tram to school and recalls, "Anne was always surrounded by other children, boys and girls, and was always the center of attention."

As Eva Schloss remembers it, "At 11 years old, she was quite a big flirt." And according to Hanneli Goslar, the attraction was mutual. "I think she had more boys as friends than girls, especially when

she was in the sixth grade and then in the first year at the Lyceum. Boys really liked her. And she always liked it a lot when all the boys paid attention to her."

To keep their gaze on her, Anne made sure to look her best. She dressed immaculately in blouses and skirts with white socks and shiny patent leather shoes, and she fussed with her shoulder-length hair. "Everyone generally liked her, and she was always the center of attention at our parties... and at school," says Hanneli. "She liked being important—that isn't a bad quality."

At the Lyceum for Girls, Margot (third from left, second row from the top) got a more traditional education.

in seventh grade, they sat next to each other in class (and sometimes even copied each other's work). "One day, a teacher grabbed Anne by the collar and put her in another class because he wanted to keep us apart," remembered Hanneli. "We had been talking too much."

Back at home, where Hanneli lived kitty-corner below the Franks at 31 Merwedeplein, the two girls were inseparable—and double trouble. When they weren't playing street games, like Voetje van de vloer ("Foot off the floor," a Dutch children's game similar to hopscotch), "we also played tricks on people," admitted Hanneli. "We'd throw water out of the window onto the people walking by.... She was always game for a prank." On Sundays, the two would get out of the neighborhood and spend the day playing at Otto Frank's Opekta office. "There was a telephone in every room, and this gave us the chance to play our favorite game:

telephoning from one room to another. That was quite an adventure."

Anne also enjoyed group activities, including pingpong. Along with four of her friends, including Hanneli and classmate Jacqueline van Maarsen, she organized their very own pingpong club, The Little Dipper Minus Two, which met for games at Ilse Wagner's house, followed by celebratory ice cream sundaes at Oase or Delphi, two of the few parlors where Jews were still allowed. Although Hanneli had always been Anne's best friend, she also had grown close to Jacqueline—who sometimes found the "outspoken" teen just a little too much to handle. "She wanted us to spend time together every day to talk or play or do homework," explained Jacqueline. "When she was alone, she was easily bored. I liked to be with her, too, but sometimes I just had other things to do." Still, Jacqueline treasured her pal. "To me, Anne was above all a dear friend." ∎

> **"SHE WAS VERY POPULAR BECAUSE SHE ALWAYS HAD IDEAS ABOUT THE GAMES THEY COULD PLAY OR THE THINGS THEY COULD GET UP TO."**
> Otto Frank,
> on his daughter Anne

HANNELI GOSLAR

EVA SCHLOSS

ANNE & EVA: FUTURE SISTERS

Little did the two 11-year-old girls playing hopscotch and marbles in "The Merry" know that one day they'd be more than just friends. Like Anne, Eva Schloss went into hiding with her family, was discovered by the Nazis and sent to Auschwitz. But unlike Anne, she survived, along with her mother, Elfriede "Fritzi" Geiringer. And when the two returned to Amsterdam after the war, they reconnected with Otto Frank, bonding over their shared grief (Fritzi had lost her husband and son in the Holocaust). From their despair, the widowed pair found a deep love, and in 1953, Otto and Fritzi married (see page 134 for more), making Eva the stepsister of Anne and Margot, albeit posthumously. "They were married for 27 years and I've never seen a happier marriage," Eva said in January 2020. "They really understood each other."

ANNE'S HIDDEN TALENT

Of the many restrictions Adolf Hitler imposed, one that came down on January 8, 1941, hit Anne particularly hard: Jews were no longer allowed to patronize movie theaters, one of her favorite pastimes. Obsessed with Hollywood, the young girl was an avid reader of *Cinema & Theater* magazine and could rattle off the names of actors and actresses in any given film (two of her favorites were Greta Garbo and Ginger Rogers). In her wildest dreams, she'd be a famous star herself one day, after the war of course. But until then, she'd have to settle for local prominence at the Merwedeplein.

After Jews were banned from attending public cultural events, families frequently got together to enjoy private recitals or readings in their homes. For his part, Otto Frank helped organize a reading circle for the neighborhood children to learn more about German literature from Anneliese Schütz, a refugee journalist who hadn't found work since emigrating from Berlin. Every week, a different household would host the group as they met to read aloud classics mostly themed around freedom, like Goethe's *Egmont*. Much to Anne's dismay, though, the 11-year-old couldn't join in with her older sister, Margot, since she no longer understood German—but soon enough, she'd be a part of something even more exciting.

That fall, Schütz helped group member Hannelore "Hansi" Klein (later, Laureen Nussbaum) direct a shoestring production of the Jewish children's play *The Princess With the Nose* to be put on inside her family's home by local youngsters under the age of 12. As soon as word got to Anne, the dramatic preteen was eager to be involved. Forgoing auditions, Laureen asked around the neighborhood to see who wanted to be in her play. Without hesitation, Anne enthusiastically agreed—and she was cast in a leading role. Although Laureen had previously recalled Anne playing the rude and opinionated princess who eats a forbidden magical cake that makes her nose grow to comical proportions, now nearly 80 years later, her memory is understandably a bit fuzzy. "I am no longer sure whether she was the queen or the princess," the 92-year-old writes in her 2019 memoir, *Shedding Our Stars*, "but I remember being struck by her vivaciousness. Yet, I did not take her quite seriously, since she was a little chatterbox."

Several times a week, the young actors met to rehearse *The Princess With the Nose* "until we had the play under control," adds Laureen, who brought the German script with her from Frankfurt, where she had performed it at school. "Anne was very lively, and she learned her lines very fast so she was very bright, clearly." Much to the amusement of Anne—who loved dressing up in fancy clothes and accessories—*The Princess With the Nose* also featured costumes tailor-made by Marianne Klein. "My mother was very handy," says Laureen, whose 11-year-old sister, Marli, was also in the play with Anne. "The king had a crown and the queen had a crown."

By mid-December at Hanukkah, they were finally ready to put on their performance in the Kleins' dining room, which doubled as a stage. Behind a dark-red curtain, Anne and her friends could hear parents, siblings and friends all buzzing in the packed adjoining living room. And she kept the audience entertained right down to the play's happy ending, when the princess pleads for forgiveness and promises to change her ways: "Good I will be and sweet as a rose; good with, but better without, this wretched nose." Was Anne nervous about her big moment? "Oh, I don't think so," says Laureen.

Anne's sixth-grade teacher witnessed that same natural confidence. Around the same time as the Merwedeplein production, she wrote and performed her very own play for her Montessori classmates. "Anne was in her element," recalled Mrs. Kuperus, who was equally impressed by the clever girl's talent as a playwright. "Of course she was full of ideas for the scripts, but since she also had no shyness and liked imitating other people, the big part fell to her. She was rather small among her classmates, but when she played the queen or the princess she suddenly seemed a good bit taller than the others."

From a young age,
Anne (in middle,
back, with
hat) and Margot
(front, in apron)
loved to dress up
in costumes.

For Anne's birthday gift, her parents allowed her to pick whichever diary she wanted.

Dear Diary

Anne's 13th birthday present changed her life—and history. Here's everything she wrote about in her diary until the Frank family went into hiding three weeks later.

IT WAS LOVE AT FIRST SIGHT FOR ANNE FRANK WHEN SHE LAID her eyes on a red plaid notebook on display in the window of a local bookstore. And just after 7 a.m. on June 12, 1942—her 13th birthday—she finally got to hold it in her hands: her very first diary. Although it was technically an autograph book, it had a cloth strap with a metal tongue that snapped into a lock—giving her all the privacy she needed to record her innermost thoughts.

Anne only had her diary for 23 days before the Franks were forced to go into hiding on July 6. In that short time, she chronicled the typical teenage musings—crushes on boys, drama with girls at school, annoying teachers, the weather—along with glimpses at the discrimination against Jews in eight entries. "I hope I will be able to confide everything to you, as I have never been able to confide in anyone," she wrote that very first day, "and I hope you will be a great source of comfort and support...I can hardly wait for those moments when I'm able to write in you."

Sunday, June 14, 1942

Two days after her birthday, Anne recalled the moment she received her diary—and all her many other gifts. "You were the first thing I saw, maybe one of my nicest presents. Then a bouquet of roses, some peonies and a potted plant. From Daddy and Mama I got a blue blouse, a game, a bottle of grape juice, which to my mind tastes a bit like wine (after all, wine is made from grapes), a puzzle, a jar of cold cream, 2.50 guilders and a gift certificate for two books. I got another book as well, *Camera Obscura* (but Margot already has it, so I exchanged mine for something else), a platter of homemade cookies (which I made myself, of course, since I've become quite an expert at baking cookies), lots of candy and a strawberry tart from Mother."

Monday, June 15, 1942

The day after her birthday party (a screening of the new *Rin Tin Tin* movie), Anne described the fun she had with her classmates, many of whom she had known since her family immigrated to Amsterdam eight years earlier. And since Kitty (the name she gave her diary) was her trusted confidante, she felt she could be candid in her true feelings about them.

Hanneli Goslar, the friend she met on her first day of kindergarten, was "a bit on the strange side.

Anne wrote mostly in Dutch, with German or English words used on occasion.

She's usually shy—outspoken at home, but reserved around other people. She blabs whatever you tell her to her mother. But she says what she thinks, and lately I've come to appreciate her a great deal." On the contrary, Anne praised "terrific" Eefje de Jong: "Though she's only twelve, she's quite the lady." And she named someone with the initials G.Z. "the prettiest girl in our class," although she was also "kind of dumb" and likely would be held back a year. (Later, Anne updated that G.Z. had graduated to the next grade "to my great surprise.")

Anne left her most biting criticism for J.R., a "detestable, sneaky, stuck-up, two-faced gossip who thinks she's so grown-up.... J. is easily offended, bursts into tears at the slightest thing and, to top it all off, is a terrible show-off. Miss J. always has to be right. She's very rich, and has a closet full of the most adorable dresses that are way too old for her. She thinks she's gorgeous, but she's not. J. and I can't stand each other."

Saturday, June 20, 1942

In her third entry, Anne opened up about herself and her family, and why Kitty was so important to her: because she didn't feel she had any friends. "Let me put it more clearly, since no one will believe that a thirteen-year-old girl is completely alone in the world. And I'm not. I have loving parents and a sixteen-year-old sister, and there are about thirty people I can call friends. I have a throng of admirers who can't keep their adoring eyes off me and who sometimes have to resort to using a broken pocket mirror to try and catch a glimpse of me in the classroom. I have a family, loving aunts and a good home. No, on the surface I seem to have everything, except my one true friend. All I think about when I'm with friends is having a good time. I can't bring myself to talk about anything but ordinary everyday things.... This is why I've started the diary."

Later that day, she returned to Kitty in a much lighter mood. She had the Frank family apartment to herself, since her parents were out and Margot had gone to play pingpong—and she wanted to talk about boys. "You're probably a little surprised to hear me talking about admirers at such a tender age," wrote Anne. "As soon as a boy asks if he can bicycle home with me and we get to talking, nine times out of ten I can be sure he'll become enamored on the spot and won't let me out of his sight for a second.... If it gets so bad that they start rambling on about 'asking Father's permission,' I swerve slightly on my bike, my schoolbag falls, and the young man feels obliged to get off his bike and hand it to me, by which time I've switched the conversation to another topic. These are the most innocent types. Of course, there are those who blow you kisses or try to take hold of your arm, but they're definitely knocking on the wrong door."

Sunday, June 21, 1942

Anne's fifth entry was all about school, namely "Mr. Keesing, the old fogey who teaches math." She explained how she often got in trouble for talking in his class—and how he punished her. "After several warnings, he assigned me extra homework. An essay on the subject 'A Chatterbox.'" The next day, when she argued with Mr. Keesing about why she hadn't done it, "he assigned me a second essay. This time it was supposed to be on 'An Incorrigible Chatterbox.' I handed it in, and Mr. Keesing had nothing to complain about for two whole classes."

When Anne still hadn't learned her lesson, however, he gave her a third assignment, "'Quack, Quack, Quack,' Said Mistress Chatterback"—which the sassy girl wrote as a poem about three baby ducks who were bitten to death by their father for quacking too much. "Keesing was trying to play a joke on me with this ridiculous subject," she wrote, "but I'd make sure the joke was on him."

Wednesday, June 24, 1942

On a particularly "sweltering" day, Anne revealed "something unexpected" happened as she walked to school. "I heard my name being called. I turned around and there was the nice boy I'd met the evening before at my friend Wilma's." (He was Wilma's second cousin, Helmuth "Hello" Silberberg.) "He asked if I would allow him to

Anne filled the pages of her first diary until December 5, 1942.

accompany me to school," added Anne. "Hello is sixteen and good at telling all kinds of funny stories."

Wednesday, July 1, 1942

Seven days later, Anne was happy to report, "Hello and I have gotten to know each other very well this past week." She also noted he had come to meet her family. Afterward, the two went for a walk—but she didn't get home until 10 minutes after the Nazi-ordered 8 p.m. curfew. "Father was furious. He said it was very wrong of me not to get home on time." Still, while Anne admired Hello, her heart belonged to another boy, Peter Schiff. "Mother is always asking me who I'm going to marry when I grow up, but I bet she'll never guess it's Peter," she revealed. "I love Peter as I've never loved anyone, and I tell myself he's only going around with all those other girls to hide his feelings for me. Maybe he thinks Hello and I are in love with each other, which we're not. He's just a friend, or as Mother puts it, a beau."

Sunday, July 5, 1942

On the last day Anne wrote in her diary before going into hiding, she coincidentally brought up that very subject. She explained how a week earlier, while on a walk with her father, he had mentioned the possibility of hiding out for the first time. Over the past year, he revealed, he'd been sending furniture and belongings to a secret place. "He sounded so serious that I felt scared," Anne wrote. But her father assured her not to worry. "'We'll take care of everything,'" she recalled he said. "'Just enjoy your carefree life while you can.' Oh, may these somber words not come true for as long as possible." ∎

Anne (second from left) stands with many of her Merwedeplein friends.

July 5, 1942, started off as a near-perfect day—but within hours, Anne's life changed forever. After graduating from the seventh grade, the 13-year-old was planning to spend that summer having fun with her friends, namely Helmuth "Hello" Silberberg, a 16-year-old Jewish boy with whom she had very recently grown close. Anne had met Hello two weeks earlier at the home of her friend Wilma, his second cousin, and it was an instant connection. The next day, June 23, she ran into him at the bike racks and he asked if he could walk her to school. "He was waiting for me again this morning," Anne wrote on June 24, "and I expect he will be from now on."

And she was right. From that moment, the two teens were inseparable. They'd spend long hours talking or going for strolls around the neighborhood. On July 1, she revealed, "He's told me a lot about his life." (Four years earlier, Hello had fled Nazi Germany by himself to live with his grandparents in Amsterdam, while a visa issue forced his parents to escape to Belgium, where they remained stuck as illegal immigrants.) "In everything he says or does, I can see that Hello is in love with me, and it's kind of nice for a change. Margot would say that Hello is a decent sort. I think so, too, but he's more than that. Mother is also full of praise: 'A good-looking boy. Nice and polite.' I'm glad he's so popular with everyone." After hanging out at Hello's home on July 4, the duo made plans to see each other the next day as well.

The morning of July 5 was a beautiful one, albeit a little too hot for Anne's liking. Before Hello came over for their pre-lunch date, she spent some time writing in her diary. She talked about her graduation ceremony just two days earlier and how her report card "wasn't too bad." As for her sister Margot's grades, Anne proudly declared, "Brilliant, as usual. If we had such a thing as 'cum laude,' she would have passed with honors, she's so smart." She concluded the diary entry by detailing a concerning conversation she had with her father a

few days earlier, in which he'd revealed plans for the family to go into hiding as fear grew that all Jews would be deported to concentration camps. As if on cue, the doorbell rang. "Hello's here," she wrote, "time to stop."

Although the two had planned to go for a stroll, they instead decided to enjoy the sunshine on the Franks' balcony. At lunchtime, Hello went home to eat with his grandparents, but promised he'd return later that afternoon. Anne then shared a midday meal with her parents and sister before retreating to the balcony to read. Her mother and sister remained in the cool indoors, while her father headed out to Weesperstraat, 2 miles away, to visit a friend in the hospital.

At 3 p.m., the doorbell rang—but it wasn't Hello. It was someone from the post office with a registered letter that required Edith's signature. Shortly after, a "very agitated" Margot joined her sister on the balcony with alarming news: "Father has received a call-up notice from the SS [Nazi paramilitary]."

A precursor to deportation, Germans had been rounding up Jews for labor service at Nazi camps, but the method wasn't always a success, as people would often get forewarning and hide out, so the Nazis began sending written summons.

Anne was stunned. "How could we let Father go to such a fate?" she asked. They wouldn't. Margot explained their mother had left to talk to Hermann van Pels, Otto's business partner, to see if they could go into hiding the next day. Over the past months, Otto and van Pels had been secretly setting up a makeshift home for both their families inside an annex connected to Opekta. As the girls anticipated Edith's return, they sat speechless. "The long wait for Mother, the heat, the suspense," recalled Anne, "all this reduced us to silence."

Suddenly, the doorbell rang again. "That's Hello," said Anne, but Margot warned, "Don't open the door!" As the boy stood outside the Franks' door, Edith returned home with van Pels in tow. It's unknown what they said to Hello, but he was turned away—likely confused by why he suddenly couldn't see his dear friend. Upstairs, Anne could hear Hello's voice as her mother and van Pels spoke to him, "and then the two of them came inside and shut the door behind them." The girls were sent to their room, where Margot shocked Anne a second time with the truth: The summons had been for her, not their father.

While they awaited for Otto, who still was unaware of what was going on back at home, the sisters began packing their most precious belongings into schoolbags. "The first thing I stuck in was this diary, and then curlers, handkerchiefs, schoolbooks, a comb and some old letters," Anne wrote days later. "Memories mean more to me than dresses."

CHAPTER 3

INTO HIDING

With Margot about to be deported to a forced labor camp in Germany, on July 6, 1942, the Franks made a mad dash to the Secret Annex, the covert space Otto had been preparing.

Race for Refuge

At dawn, the Franks made a mad dash for the Secret Annex, anxious to reach their destination before the Nazis could catch them.

A revolving
bookcase that
opened like a door
concealed the
annex's entrance.

The Franks' final morning before going into hiding was a dreary one:

THE HUMID SUMMER RAIN WAS SUFFOCATING—YET IT provided protection from Nazis who would normally be patrolling the streets. Moments before 7:30 a.m., Otto's trusted employee Miep Gies arrived with her bicycle to escort Margot to Opekta's annex first, with Otto, Edith and Anne Frank to follow on their own. "No sooner had I reached the front stoop than the door of the Franks' apartment opened and Margot emerged," recalled Miep, then 33. "Mr. and Mrs. Frank were inside, and Anne, wide-eyed in a nightgown, hung back inside the doorway. I could tell that Margot was wearing layers of clothing. Mr. and Mrs. Frank looked at me. Their eyes pierced mine…. 'Go,' Mr.

Frank instructed us, taking a look up and down the square. 'Go now.'"

At once, Margot and Miep set out for 263 Prinsengracht, 2 miles away, maintaining a relaxed yet steady pace "in order to appear like two everyday working girls on their way to work on a Monday morning," explained Miep in her book, *Anne Frank Remembered.* "We had not said one word. We both knew that from the moment we'd mounted our bicycles we'd become criminals. There we were, a Christian and a Jew without the yellow star, riding on an illegal bicycle. And at a time when the Jew was ordered to report for a forced-labor brigade about to leave for parts unknown in Hitler's Germany. Margot's face showed no intimidation. She betrayed nothing of what she was feeling inside. Suddenly we'd become two allies against the might of the German beast among us."

Once they reached Prinsengracht, Miep was relieved to see it was empty of pedestrians. She unlocked Opekta's door and ushered Margot off the street. Although they had reached their destination without being caught, Margot wouldn't be truly safe until she was secured inside the annex. By this time, though, employees could be arriving for work. Surely, the sight of their boss' daughter—soaking wet

The Secret Annex was located on the Prinsengracht, one of the four main canals in Amsterdam.

Otto Frank moved his business to 263 Prinsengracht in 1940, 300 years after the building had been built.

Annexes were
added to the
buildings along
Prinsengracht
to create a
live-work space.

FIRST DAY IN HIDING

With Edith and Margot in shock from the morning's stressful escape, it was up to Anne and Otto to make the annex feel like a real home. "All the cardboard boxes that had been sent to the office in the last few months were piled on the floors and beds," Anne recounted in her diary four days later on July 10. "The small room was filled from floor to ceiling with linens. If we wanted to sleep in properly made beds that night, we had to get going and straighten up the mess. Mother and Margot were unable to move a muscle. They lay down on their bare mattresses, tired, miserable and I don't know what else. But Father and I, the two cleaner-uppers in the family, started in right away." All throughout the day, Anne and Otto unpacked boxes, filled cupboards, hammered nails and straightened up the mess "until we fell exhausted into our clean beds at night. We hadn't eaten a hot meal all day, but we didn't care; Mother and Margot were too tired and keyed up to eat, and Father and I were too busy."

and visibly on the verge of crumbling—would give away that something was afoot. Silently, Miep led the 16-year-old up a wooden stairway to the annex entrance. "Margot was now like someone stunned, in shock," remembered Miep. "As she opened the door, I gripped her arm to give her courage. Still, we said nothing. She disappeared behind the door, and I took my place in the front office."

Miep pretended to work, and anxiously awaited Otto, Edith and Anne. Before the Franks left Merwedeplein 37-2, they staged the scene to look like the Jewish family had left in a hurry to hide out with Otto's family in Switzerland: They stripped the beds, left breakfast untouched on the dining room table and put out a pound of meat in the kitchen for their cat Moortje, "the only living creature I said goodbye to," Anne sadly reflected. Otto even paid the rent for the next year in advance, assuming the war would be over soon and they'd return home.

Since Jews had been banned from using public transportation, the trio made the dangerous trek on foot—while wearing multiple layers of clothing in the steamy summer rain. Anne was weighed down by two undershirts, three pairs of underwear, a dress with a shirt over it, a jacket, two pairs of stockings, heavy shoes, all topped off with a hat, scarf and raincoat. "I was suffocating even before we left the house," she said, "but no one bothered to ask me how I felt." The trio each carried shopping bags filled to the brim with various items, to a destination still unknown to the 13-year-old. "Where would we hide?" Anne wondered. "In the city? In the country? In a house? In a shack? When, where, how...? These were questions I wasn't allowed to ask, but they still kept running through my mind."

An hour later, she got her answer when they arrived at the four-story brick building along Prinsengracht, one of Amsterdam's main canals. Miep quickly brought them inside and up to the third floor. At the landing, there was a set of doors: On the left, a portal leading to a storage area in the front of the building; on the right, another that went to a vacant wing in the rear. Miep opened the latter and Otto, Edith and Anne all hurried inside,

where they found Margot anxiously waiting. It was the first time Anne had ever seen the inside of the annex, and she couldn't believe her eyes.

For months, her father had been moving furniture and food into the hiding place; it was scattered everywhere. When Miep went upstairs that afternoon to check on the Franks, she noticed Anne and Otto were busy working "to create some order out of the multitude of objects, pushing, carrying, clearing." Edith and Margot, meanwhile, "were like lost people, drained of blood, in conditions of complete lethargy. They appeared as though they couldn't move" (see sidebar, opposite page). The helper offered to bring the Franks some food items to get them through their first night—bread, butter and milk—which they graciously accepted.

"The situation was very upsetting," Miep described years later. "I wanted to leave the family alone together. I couldn't begin to imagine what they must be feeling to have walked away from everything they owned in the world—their home; a lifetime of gathered possessions; Anne's little cat, Moortje. Keepsakes from the past. And friends. They had simply closed the door of their lives and had vanished from Amsterdam." ∎

WHY MARGOT TRAVELED BY BICYCLE

In June 1942, Jews were ordered to turn in their bicycles, in perfect condition and with spare tires, to authorities. But the Franks did not comply. They gave Edith's to Christian friends for safekeeping and hid Margot's inside their home in case of an emergency; just weeks later, it came in handy as their elder daughter raced to the annex. Once she safely got there, however, the illegal wheels also went into hiding: Victor Kugler, one of the helpers (see page 70), "arrived at work and took Margot's bicycle somewhere that I didn't know," Miep Gies later revealed.

Who Were

DURING THE HOLOCAUST, AN ESTIMATED 28,000 DUTCH JEWS went into hiding, but very few had a network of loyal helpers as the fugitives living inside the Secret Annex. Four of Otto Frank's longtime employees—Miep Gies, Victor Kugler, Johannes Kleiman and Bep Voskuijl, as well as a select few close to them—were responsible for the day-to-day care of the Jews, a commitment that also put their own lives on the line.

Kleiman, Opekta's managing director and Otto's right-hand man, was the person who first suggested the unused annex attached to the rear of their office building—which had only one entrance—would be an ideal hiding place for the Franks should the time come, and he even helped Otto covertly move belongings out of their apartment. Kleiman's brother Willy ran a cleaning business and he regularly stopped by the family's

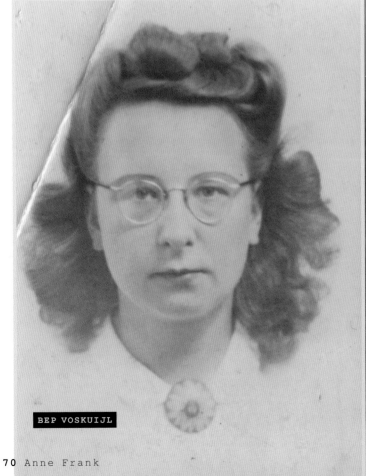

BEP VOSKUIJL

JOHAN VOSKUIJL

The Helpers

home to pick up one or two pieces of furniture to be "refurbished," but instead would bring them to the annex, where dishes, bedding and food were also being stockpiled.

For more than two years, the helpers pulled double duty, juggling their jobs at Opekta while caring for everyone hiding in the annex. In order to pull it off, they divvied up the responsibilities: Miep and Bep, a typist, oversaw the daily

Otto's trusted employees and friends—Bep and Johan Voskuijl, Jan and Miep Gies, Johannes Kleiman and Victor Kugler—were responsible for the Franks' survival in the annex.

JAN GIES

necessities, like food and clothing, while Kleiman and Kugler managed the finances for it all. Every morning, Miep, who started out as Otto's secretary, went grocery shopping with ration coupons at a few trusted vendors for meat and fresh produce. "Miep is just like a pack mule," said Anne, "she fetches and carries so much." Milk and bread were delivered daily for Opekta employees, with enough requested for eight extra people, which Bep then smuggled up to the annex on her lunch break.

Kugler, who also supplied the hidden Jews with newspapers and magazines, generated extra money for them by not entering sales of spices in the official books. A serious man, he often worried about the safety of those in hiding, and a few weeks after they moved in, he tasked Bep's father, Opekta warehouse manager Johan Voskuijl, with building a revolving bookcase to disguise the annex's door. As for Kleiman, a confidant Otto first employed at the Michael Frank Bank in the early 1920s, he

JOHANNES KLEIMAN

VICTOR KUGLER

served as the main point of contact and ensured the delivery of encrypted messages from the Franks to their concerned loved ones in Switzerland.

Over the years, the five helpers (plus Miep's husband, Jan, who brought library books) did more than provide food and shelter—they became part of the family. "They come upstairs every day and talk to the men about business and politics, to the women about food and wartime difficulties and to the children about books and newspapers," said Anne. "They put on their most cheerful expressions, bring flowers and gifts for birthdays and holidays and are always ready to do what they can."

Anne grew especially close to 23-year-old Bep, the youngest of the helpers, who often ate dinner with everyone in the annex. Once, she convinced Bep to spend the night, but Bep hardly slept. "I was terrified," she revealed. "Every time I heard a tree creaking in the October wind or a car driving along the canal, I grew afraid. I was grateful when morning came and I was able to get back to work."

On the weekends, Kleiman brought his wife, Johanna, by the annex to visit, and Anne was always curious to talk to her about life in the outside world. "She would ask about Corrie, our daughter," said Kleiman. "She wanted to know what Corrie was doing, what boyfriends she had, what was happening at the hockey club, whether Corrie had fallen in love. And she would stand there, thin, in her washed-out clothes, her face snow-white, for they had not been out of doors for so long. My wife would always bring something for her, a pair of sandals or a piece of cloth."

As for Kugler, he kept the secret of those in hiding from his wife, Laura, so he had no one with whom to share his fears—and the anxiety ate away at him. "The responsibility Mr. Kugler had taken on weighed very heavy on him and he lived under constant pressure," Otto later said. Anne noticed it too, writing in her diary: "The enormous responsibility for the eight of us is sometimes so much for him, that he can hardly talk from pent-up nerves and strain."

The helpers risked their own lives for those in the annex, and their sacrifice was not lost on the ones they protected, especially their grateful boss. "They were fully aware of the dangerous task they would be taking upon themselves in doing so," Otto said years later. "By Nazi law, everyone helping Jews was severely punished and risked being put into prison, being deported or even shot." But to the helpers, it was never an option to turn their backs. "We did our human duty," insisted Miep in 1998, "helping people in need." ∎

MIEP GIES

The dining area
was adjacent
to Hermann and
Auguste van Pels'
sleeping quarters.

Life in Secret

Here's how the eight Jewish fugitives passed the 761 long days (and nights) inside their cramped 500-square-foot hidden world.

SEVEN DAYS AFTER THE FRANKS WENT INTO HIDING, THREE more people joined them inside the annex: Otto's business partner Hermann van Pels, his wife, Auguste, and their 16-year-old son, Peter. The family had planned to move in on July 14, 1942, but as the Nazis prepared to deport 4,000 Jews from German-occupied Amsterdam, "they decided it would be safer to leave a day too early than a day too late," Anne explained in her diary. Over the course of July 15, 16 and 17, two trains, each carrying 700 Jews, left the Netherlands, bound for the Auschwitz concentration camp in Poland.

The Franks and the van Pelses were old friends, so Anne was looking forward to their company. From their very first day, all seven ate meals together like "one big family." They lived like one, too, in the three-level space: The Franks took the first floor, with Otto and Edith in one room and Anne and Margot crammed into another only as wide as its window. A steep staircase went up to Hermann and Auguste's quarters (also the common area during the day), while Peter slept nearby in a passageway to the attic that could barely fit a narrow bed. Everyone shared the lone bathroom on the Franks' floor. It had a sink with running water and a toilet, which could only be flushed in the evenings once the Opekta employees below went home.

In the cramped 500-square-foot space, it didn't take long for the seven friends to grate on each other's nerves. The van Pelses were an eclectic trio: Know-it-all Hermann, moody Auguste and withdrawn Peter frequently (and explosively) clashed. Quite the contrary, the Franks were mostly easygoing. Within weeks, Anne and 44-year-old Hermann were "always at loggerheads," she reported in her diary. The two matriarchs were also warring over their respective families sharing linens and china—especially after Anne broke one of "unbearable" Auguste's soup bowls. As for their son, Anne added, "I don't think Peter's gotten any nicer. He's an obnoxious boy who lies around on his bed all day, only rousing himself to do a little carpentry work before returning to his nap. What a dope!"

On the plus side, there was plenty of food to eat in the annex, at least in the beginning: three meals a day consisting of meat, fresh vegetables and fruit, beans, milk and bread. In the first three months, Anne gained a healthy 19 pounds to weigh 96, while Margot was 132. Their rations were so bountiful, in fact, that the seven felt there was enough room for them to welcome one more Jew in need of refuge. They went over a list of possibilities, "trying to come up with a single person who would blend in well with our extended family," Anne explained that November. They settled on Fritz Pfeffer, a German dentist who lost his practice when he emigrated. Their reasoning was twofold: "We'll ask him to bring along something to fill cavities with," noted Anne, who became his roommate (Margot slept on a cot into Otto and Edith's room). "To be honest, I'm not exactly delighted at having a stranger use my things, but you have to make sacrifices for a good cause, and I'm glad I can make this small one."

During the days, when they were required to remain silent, each person occupied their time with sedentary activities, such as reading, knitting, sewing, peeling potatoes and learning English. Miep Gies and her husband, Jan, brought over library books every week, as did Johannes Kleiman from his own personal collection. (Victor Kugler supplied Anne with issues of her favorite *Cinema & Theater* magazine). "We're like a bunch of little kids with a present," she described. "Ordinary people don't know how much books can mean to

Extra food, like canned goods and beans, were stored in the annex's attic.

someone who's cooped up. Our only diversions are reading, studying and listening to the radio."

That fall, just as the school year began outside the annex, Anne, Margot and Peter kept busy with their studies. Anne focused on French, history (her favorite subject) and "wretched" math, the latter of which she refused to do every day. "Daddy thinks it's awful too. I'm almost better at it than he

"BORING" SATURDAYS & "MISERABLE" SUNDAYS

Most people look forward to the weekends, but in the annex, Saturdays and Sundays were far from enjoyable. Although they were allowed to freely wander around 263 Prinsengracht, since the warehouse workers were away until Monday, there were still people living in the surrounding buildings who could potentially spot one of the Jewish fugitives.

"Since the curtains are drawn on Saturday afternoon, we scrub ourselves in the dark," revealed Anne, "while the one who isn't in the bath looks out the window through a chink in the curtains and gazes in wonder at the endlessly amusing people." The remainder of the day was often spent making meatballs or shelling peas—for hours on end. "It's a horror for an impatient teenager like me," Anne complained. "The monotony was killing me."

There was one upside to Saturdays though: When Miep Gies came to visit, she always brought five library books. And for the chatterbox, another bright spot was being able to talk. In March 1944, after a 90-minute conversation with Peter, she gushed, "This is the first Saturday in months that hasn't been tiresome, dreary and boring.... We talked until quarter to one."

Worse yet were Sundays. Although everyone preferred to sleep in, Fritz Pfeffer got up "at the crack of dawn to exercise for 10 minutes" in his shared room with Anne. "The torment seems to last for hours since the chairs I use to make my bed longer are constantly being jiggled under my sleepy head." He would then stomp up and down the stairs before heading to the bathroom, "where he devotes a whole hour to washing himself." Once back in the bedroom, the dentist spent another 15 minutes praying, which Anne described as "a terrible sight to behold" as he rocked back and forth the entire time. From there, the rest of the day didn't get much better: The hours seemed to drag by, as activities alternated between relaxing (eating, bathing and napping) and backbreaking work (two hours of "scrubbing, sweeping and washing").

"My nerves often get the better of me, especially on Sundays; that's when I really feel miserable," Anne moaned in the pages of her diary. "The atmosphere is stifling, sluggish, leaden. Outside, you don't hear a single bird, and a deathly, oppressive silence hangs over the house and clings to me as if it were going to drag me into the deepest regions of the underworld.... I wander from room to room, climb up and down the stairs and feel like a songbird whose wings have been ripped off and who keeps hurling itself against the bars of its dark cage. 'Let me out, where there's fresh air and laughter!' a voice within me cries."

is, though in fact neither of us is any good, so we always have to call on Margot's help." The father and daughter also worked together on the Frank family tree, "and he tells me something about each person as we go along." As for Margot, the honors student devoured everything she could: "Correspondence courses in English, French and Latin, shorthand in English, German and Dutch, trigonometry, solid geometry, mechanics, physics, chemistry, algebra, geometry, English literature, French literature, German literature, Dutch literature, bookkeeping, geography, modern history, biology, economics; reads everything, preferably on religion and medicine," according to Anne.

A typical day began at 6:45 a.m., when Hermann's alarm clock went off and woke up everyone in the

"I MUST UPHOLD MY IDEALS, FOR PERHAPS THE TIME WILL COME WHEN I SHALL BE ABLE TO CARRY THEM OUT."

The Diary of Anne Frank, July 15, 1944

annex. All had their allotted time in the lavatory, located next to Anne and Pfeffer's room, and first up was Mr. van Pels. After his half-hour, next it was the dentist's turn. "Alone at last," sighed Anne, who'd then remove the blackout screen from the window to let the sunshine in, as she listened for three gentle taps on the floor that signaled her breakfast (usually hot cereal) was ready. At 8:30 a.m., Opekta warehouse workers started filing in below on the ground floor, which meant everyone in the annex could not make a sound. "No running water, no flushing toilet, no walking around, no noise whatsoever," explained Anne. But once Miep, Kleiman, Kugler and Bep Voskuijl showed up at 9 a.m., the fugitives were allowed to walk around in socks, as the helpers made their own hubbub on the second floor, masking any mysterious sounds that came from the supposedly empty annex.

Once the clock struck 12:30 p.m., the warehouse workers left for lunch, and that meant those in the annex were free to make a little noise. For Auguste, that was vacuuming her only rug. Anne always looked forward to this time because it was when the helpers, particularly Miep and Bep, came upstairs to eat (typically soup, and dessert if they were lucky) and socialize until 1:45 p.m., when they headed back to the offices before the other employees returned. "What comes next is the quietest hour of the day"—when most everyone took a nap.

Without any disturbances, Anne spent this time reading (Hans Christian Andersen fairy tales and Greek mythology were some of her favorites) or writing at the desk she shared with Pfeffer in their room. She communicated so much with "Kitty,"

Anne decorated
her room with
photos of
her favorite
Hollywood stars.

whom she described as "a nice 14-year-old girl," that by December 1942, the diary's pages were already filled. Thanks to notebooks she received from Margot, as well as loose sheets of paper provided to her by Miep and Bep, she was able to resume her passion. "Although everyone knew that she was writing, she never wrote when other people were present," said Miep. "As I heard from Mr. Frank, the diary was a constant companion for Anne, and also a source of teasing by the others. How was she finding so much to write about? Anne's cheeks went pink when she was teased." For

safekeeping, she kept her diary and notebooks in her father's old leather briefcase next to his bed.

All day, Anne waited for evening. At 5:45 p.m., after the final Opekta shift left, everyone went downstairs. Anne and Margot usually did clerical work that Miep and Bep had left for them, exercised or listened to the radio. After three hours, it was time to go back upstairs. "Bedtime always begins in the annex with an enormous hustle and bustle," Anne wrote. "Chairs are shifted, beds pulled out, blankets unfolded—nothing stays where it is during the daytime." Once Peter was done with

Edith Frank and Auguste van Pels cooked all the meals in the annex's kitchen.

the bathroom, it was Anne's turn at 9:30 p.m. Her nightly beauty ritual: "I wash myself from head to toe, and more often than not I find a tiny flea floating in the sink (only during the hot months, weeks or days). I brush my teeth, curl my hair, manicure my nails and dab peroxide on my upper lip to bleach the black hairs—all this in less than half an hour." At 10 p.m., Anne put back the blackout screen she had taken down that morning. Another day had come and gone.

When they first sought refuge in the annex, everyone believed it would be temporary. Nearly a year later, however, they were still in hiding—and feeling the effects of the war-torn world: During the Dutch famine, their own rations were meager. "Our food is terrible," Anne complained on April 27, 1943. "Breakfast consists of plain unbuttered bread and ersatz coffee. For the last two weeks lunch has been either spinach or cooked lettuce with huge potatoes that have a rotten, sweetish taste." As fresh food became more scarce, they relied on their emergency supply of canned foods, condensed milk, rice and oatmeal.

Their health diminished along with the quality of their food. The Frank girls were especially prone to illness. Margot suffered from chronic bronchitis and her coughing raised fears she'd be heard. To quiet her at night (and aid sleep), she was given large doses of codeine. Anne also frequently came down with colds and flus. "I get dizzy just thinking about all the cures I've been subjected to: sweating out the fever, steam treatment, wet compresses, dry compresses, hot drinks, swabbing my throat, lying still, heating pad, hot-water bottles, lemonade and, every two hours, the thermometer."

Despite Anne's hunger, boredom and frustration with being trapped inside, eventually there was one positive aspect to life in the annex: Peter. In early 1944, as the 14-year-old hit puberty, she started to look at the shy boy with piercing blue eyes in a different way. "My life now has some object and I have something to look forward to," she wrote on February 18. "Everything has become more pleasant." ∎

A TYPICAL DAY

6:45 A.M. The van Pels' alarm clock sounds, waking everyone up.

7:00 A.M. Anne gets up and removes the blackout screens from the windows, and everyone takes turns using the shared bathroom. Once washed and dressed, everyone stows away their bedding so the annex feels more spacious.

8:30 A.M. Opekta employees arrive for work in the warehouse below, meaning everyone in the annex must remain quiet.

9:00 A.M. The helpers start their day in offices located above the warehouse, making noises less suspicious, so annex residents are now allowed to walk around in socks. The morning is spent reading or studying.

12:45 P.M. With the warehouse workers home for lunch, a few of the helpers come upstairs to the annex to eat and share news.

1:45 P.M. The helpers return to their offices, while those in the annex spend the remainder of the afternoon napping, reading or studying.

4:00 P.M. After a cup of coffee, dinner preparations begin.

5:30 P.M. Warehouse workers end their shifts and go home, allowing those in the annex freedom to move around as they please and even go downstairs.

9:00 P.M. Sleeping preparations begin: Daytime furniture is replaced with bedding and everyone takes shifts in the bathroom.

Sundays Everyone in the annex sleeps until 8:00 a.m. and then take turns using the bathroom. At 11:30, it's breakfast, followed by two hours of "scrubbing, sweeping and washing" until a 2:00 p.m. nap. Before dinner, they usually listen to a concert on the radio. Anne considers Sunday the most miserable day.

ALLIES & ENEMIES: WHO GOT ALONG INSIDE

FRITZ PFEFFER

AUGUSTE VAN PELS

Throughout the two years cooped up together, it was an emotional roller coaster for the eight Jews, who oftentimes took it out on each other.

Within weeks of moving in, Hermann and Auguste van Pels were already at each other's throats—and it mostly stayed that way. "I've never seen anything like it, since Mother and Father wouldn't dream of shouting at each other like that," Anne wrote on September 2, 1942, about a "terrible fight" between the married couple. In that same entry, she detailed a violent clash after Peter disobeyed his parents and read a forbidden book "about women." When Hermann caught his son with it, there was "a slap, a whack and a tug-of-war," resulting in Peter refusing to leave his room for three days, until Otto eventually played peacemaker. Although Auguste defended her son that time, she had her own tussles with him, including one that turned physical when she tried to give him a haircut. She made such a fuss to her husband, he dragged Peter from the attic and gave him "a merciless scolding."

The Franks had their share of problems, "even though our family never has the same kind of outbursts they have upstairs," insisted Anne, who was regularly at odds with her sister and mother. But when Auguste butted her

HERMANN VAN PELS

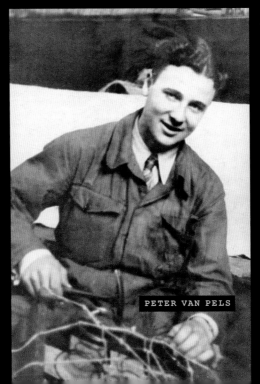

PETER VAN PELS

nose in their business, Anne couldn't help but snap back with a "saucy" reply—and her parents jumped into the fray to defend her. "If I take a small helping of a vegetable I loathe and eat potatoes instead, the van [Pelses], especially Mrs. van [Pels], can't get over how spoiled I am.... This is always how her tirades begin and end: 'If Anne were my daughter...' Thank goodness I'm not." Otto took exception to Auguste's judgment. "I think Anne is very well brought up," he retorted. "At least she's learned not to respond to your interminable sermons."

While things only worsened between Anne and Auguste—whom she despised for flirting with her father—she did turn a corner with Margot and Edith. But soon enough, she had a new enemy in Fritz Pfeffer. Eleven days after "His Excellency" moved in to the annex, he "turned out to be an old-fashioned disciplinarian and preacher of unbearably long sermons on manners," complained Anne, the recipient of his wrath.

Although Pfeffer was 40 years older, the two bickered like children, mostly over sharing the desk in their room where Anne liked to study. On one occasion, Anne asked Pfeffer for more time at the desk. "I already sit there every day from two-thirty to four while [Pfeffer] takes a nap," she noted, "so it seemed a reasonable request." But Pfeffer said no, which led to a fight in which he scoffed to Anne, "Mythology—what kind of work is that? Reading and knitting don't count either! I use that table and I'm not going to give it up!" After Otto got involved, Pfeffer sulked.

Anne wasn't the only one on the receiving end of Pfeffer's silent treatments. After thieves broke into Opekta's warehouse, security measures were tightened and Hermann declared the windows could no longer be opened at night, which ignited a furious shouting match. When Otto intervened, Pfeffer insulted him, too. "Not one of us knows what he said," wrote Anne, "but it must have been pretty awful." For 10 days, the dentist didn't speak to anyone—but

finally apologized the night before his birthday. At his celebration, everyone gave him a thoughtful gift (a bottle of good wine from the Franks), and in return, he treated them all to an egg.

Still, the truce was short-lived: Weeks later, he quarreled with the Franks over the division of butter and backed the van Pelses when they balked at baking a spice cake for Victor Kugler's birthday when they couldn't have one themselves. The new alliance took an odd turn when Pfeffer and Auguste openly flirted with each other and even shared a kiss.

Just as it was before they went into hiding, Anne remained closest to her father, and she was heartbroken when he disapproved of her spending time with Peter. She wrote him a letter, but the teen's emotions got the best of her: "I'm an independent person, and I don't feel I need to account to you for my actions." Deeply hurt, when Otto relayed his feelings to Anne, she was distraught. "This is the worst thing I've ever done in my entire life," she mourned. "What I'm most ashamed of is the way Father has forgiven me; he said he's going to throw the letter in the stove, and he's being so nice to me now, as if he were the one who'd done something wrong."

As they came upon the two-year mark in the annex, everyone understandably was at their wits' end. Auguste, overcome by fear they'd be discovered, was in the worst shape, and took it out on them all. "She's jealous that Peter confides in me and not in her, offended that [Pfeffer] doesn't respond sufficiently to her flirtations and afraid her husband's going to squander all the fur-coat money on tobacco," Anne revealed on June 16, 1944. "She quarrels, curses, cries, feels sorry for herself, laughs and starts all over again." And one by one, the others were affected, too: "Even worse, Peter's becoming insolent, Mr. van [Pels] irritable and Mother cynical. Yes, everyone's in quite a state! There's only one thing you need to remember: Laugh at everything and forget everybody else!"

Tour the Annex

Take a closer look at the tight quarters that Anne and the seven other refugees shared for more than two years.

THERE'S MORE TO 263 PRINSENGRACHT THAN meets the eye. Opekta, Otto Frank's business, was located in the four-story front section and featured a warehouse, three offices, a stockroom, a kitchen and the attic. Behind that is the annex, which had been used as a laboratory to experiment with fruit jams until Otto decided to turn it into his family's secret hiding place. "I don't think I'll ever feel at home in this house, but that doesn't mean I hate it," Anne wrote in her diary just five days after they moved in. "It may be damp and lopsided, but there's probably not a more comfortable hiding place in all of Amsterdam. No, in all of Holland." ■

263 PRINSENGRACHT

MAP TO THE ROOMS

1 BOOKCASE The entrance to the Secret Annex was through a door concealed by a revolving bookcase.

2 BATHROOM Back out in the main entrance, the first door on the right was the annex's sole bathroom, which had a sink and a toilet.

3 OTTO, EDITH & MARGOT'S ROOM Once past the bookcase and through the entrance, the first door to the left led to the bedroom of Anne's parents, Otto and Edith Frank, and her sister, Margot.

4 ANNE & FRITZ'S ROOM A door in the corner of the bathroom led to a small bedroom that belonged to Anne and Fritz Pfeffer.

5 HERMANN & AUGUSTE'S ROOM From the main floor, a steep staircase led right into "a large, light and spacious room" that served many purposes.

6 PETER'S ROOM Off the van Pels' bedroom was a tiny passageway to the attic, which was converted into a room for their teenage son. Anne and Peter spent much of their time in his room talking.

7 ATTIC In the middle of Peter's room was a ladder that led up to the attic, which was primarily used to store food, like potatoes and beans. There was also a clothesline to dry laundry. The attic was the place people would head to if they wanted to be alone or have a private conversation.

The Anne Frank House temporarily refurbished the annex's rooms for the 1998 documentary *Remembering Anne Frank*.

ATTIC

STOCK ROOM

1

2

3

4

5

6

7

STAIRCASE

OFFICE

TOILET

KITCHEN

PRIVATE OFFICE

WAREHOUSE

WAREHOUSE

Until Anne (far right) fell for Peter, she assumed he was in love with Margot.

Sister

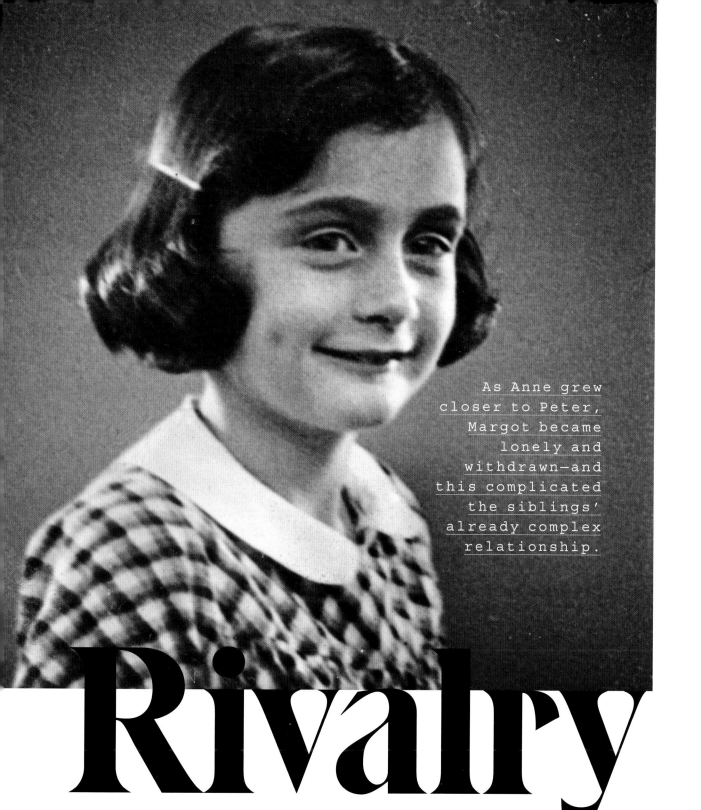

As Anne grew closer to Peter, Margot became lonely and withdrawn—and this complicated the siblings' already complex relationship.

Rivalry

BEFORE GOING INTO HIDING, MARGOT AND ANNE OFTEN caught the eyes of boys their age. The extroverted Anne, though, was the one who enjoyed the attention much more and shamelessly flirted right back with her many young suitors around the neighborhood. Yet when Peter van Pels moved into the annex, Anne hardly gave him a second glance, describing him as "a shy, awkward boy whose company won't amount to much."

Anne didn't appreciate Peter's clumsy attempts at affection, either. "He often pats me on the cheek, which I don't like," she wrote about complaining to his parents. "They asked me in a typically grown-up way whether I could ever learn to love Peter like a brother, since he loves me like a sister. 'Oh, no!' I said, but what I was thinking was, 'Oh, ugh!' Just imagine.... Boys who aren't used to being around girls are like that."

But over time, Peter matured—and Anne had a change of heart. In January 1944, after 18 months of living together, she began to see him in a new light. "My longing for someone to talk to has become so unbearable that I somehow took it into my head to select Peter for this role," she revealed in her diary. At the time, the 17-year-old was going through an obsessive crossword puzzle phase and he spent all day holed up alone in his room, until Anne popped by one night and offered to help solve one. "It gave me a wonderful feeling when I looked into his dark blue eyes and saw how bashful

DID MARGOT HAVE FEELINGS FOR PETER?

Just as Anne and Peter were getting closer, "a shadow has fallen on my happiness," Anne revealed in her diary on March 20, 1944. "For a long time I've had the feeling that Margot likes Peter. Just how much I don't know, but the whole situation is very unpleasant. Now every time I go see Peter I'm hurting her, without meaning to. The funny thing is that she hardly lets it show. I know I'd be insanely jealous, but Margot just says I shouldn't feel sorry for her. 'I think it's so awful that you've become the odd one out,' I added. 'I'm used to that,' she replied, somewhat bitterly."

The next day, though, Margot changed her tune, and in a letter to her sister she opened up about her true feelings. "When I said I wasn't jealous of you, I wasn't being entirely honest," she wrote to Anne. "The situation is this: I'm not jealous of either you or Peter. I'm just sorry I haven't found anyone with whom to share my thoughts and feelings, and I'm not likely to in the near future." Although she wished Anne and Peter "will both be able to place your trust in each other," Margot went on to explain why she and Peter would never work, in a somewhat backhanded insult to Anne. "I'd need to feel very close to a person before I could share my thoughts.... For this reason it would have to be someone I felt was intellectually superior to me, and that isn't the case with Peter. But I can imagine your feeling close to him."

In Anne's response, she thanked Margot for her kindness in the matter, but admitted she didn't feel right about it. "If there's anything you still want to discuss, please write, because it's easier for me to say what I mean on paper than face-to-face."

Margot did just that two days later—again, with a somewhat passive-aggressive tone. "I have the unpleasant feeling that your conscience bothers you whenever you go to Peter's to work or talk; there's really no reason for that. In my heart, I know there's someone who deserves my trust (as I do his), and I wouldn't be able to tolerate Peter in his place."

Despite their differences, Anne and Margot had a close relationship.

my unexpected visit had made him. I could read his innermost thoughts, and in his face I saw a look of helplessness and uncertainty as to how to behave, and at the same time a flicker of awareness of his masculinity. I saw his shyness, and I melted." That night as she lay in bed, Anne thought, "I've made up my mind to visit Peter more often and, somehow, get him to talk to me."

Just as she hoped, the two connected, spending endless hours alone in Peter's room or upstairs in the attic bonding over intimate conversations and innocent cuddles. As Anne's crush developed into infatuation, she paid more attention to her appearance: The 14-year-old trimmed her nails, bleached the fuzz above her lip with peroxide and curled her hair. During this awakening, Anne's diary is filled with page after page about Peter, a welcome distraction as emotions in the annex reflected the rise of Nazi raids throughout Amsterdam. "Morning, noon and night, I look forward to seeing Peter," she gushed. "Oh, I'm so happy! I wonder if he's going to fall in love with me after all?"

Like Peter, Margot was quite withdrawn in the annex. But while his relationship with Anne helped him come out of his shell, it seemed to push the older sister further into hers—and Anne felt torn between happiness and Margot's sorrow. "It bothers me that Margot has to sit downstairs all by herself, while I'm upstairs enjoying Peter's company. But what can I do about it? I wouldn't mind it if she came, but she'd just be the odd one out, sitting there like a lump on a log." Peter did eventually invite Margot to join him and Anne in the attic. "Whether he really means it or is just

saying it out of politeness, I don't know," mused his young paramour, who must have felt a pang of jealousy, even though she insisted to Margot, "You're welcome to join us."

Margot did occasionally join them, although it felt awkward to be the third wheel. Anne sensed the tension, too—and confronted her sister about her suspicions (see sidebar on page 88 for more). Margot insisted that she looked at Peter only as a brother, not a boyfriend. "We've been sending out feelers, and a brotherly and sisterly affection may or may not develop at some later date, but it's certainly not reached that stage yet," she told Anne. "So there's no need for you to feel sorry for me. Now that you've found companionship, enjoy it as much as you can."

Anne took that advice to heart. Not long after learning what Margot thought of Peter, she shared her first kiss with him. During one of their nightly chats in his room, the boy made the first move: He put his arm around Anne, who reciprocated "so that I was nearly engulfed by him," she excitedly recounted on April 16. "We've sat like this on other occasions, but never so close as we were last night. He held me firmly against him, my left side against his chest; my heart had already begun to beat faster, but there was more to come...he caressed my cheek and arm, a bit clumsily, and played with my hair. Most of the time our heads were touching." At 9:30 p.m., when it was time to go to sleep, Peter seized the moment, albeit a bit awkwardly. "Before we went downstairs, he gave me a kiss, through my hair, half on my left cheek and half on my ear."

With her first kiss achieved, Anne felt so grown-up—and much more advanced than her older, straight-laced sister. "Not even fifteen and already so independent—that's a little

Margot was a doting older sister when she and Anne were young, but as teens the two became more like peers.

hard for other people to understand. I'm pretty sure Margot would never kiss a boy unless there was some talk of an engagement or marriage. Neither Peter nor I has any such plans. I'm also sure that Mother never touched a man before she met Father."

For Anne's 15th birthday on June 12, Peter wanted to give her something special. But as he was stuck in the annex, he enlisted Miep Gies for help, which surprised her since he almost never initiated conversation with her. Miep recalled how Peter pressed a few coins into her hand and "asked me if I could find some pretty flowers for Anne.... As he stood there, I saw how strong-looking he was, how curly his brown hair was. Sweet boy, I thought, impressed by Peter's new tenderhearted side." Anne was, too. In her diary, she listed all of her birthday gifts, and saved the best for last: "Peter gave me a lovely bouquet of peonies."

But with the excitement came confusion. Anne wondered if the two would have fallen for each other were it not for the annex. And

"I'M GOING TO TELL [PETER] YOU'RE ALSO VERY FOND OF HIM. I DON'T KNOW WHAT PETER THINKS OF YOU, BUT I'LL ASK HIM WHEN THE TIME COMES."

Anne, in a letter to Margot

as liberation seemed imminent, it was a concern she wanted to address—but first, she opened up about it to Margot. "It can't be much longer before Peter and I will have to decide whether to go back to the way we were or do something else," she told her sister. "I don't know how it'll turn out; I can't see any farther than the end of my nose." But she did know one thing: There was a great love out there for Margot, too. "Keep your spirits up!" Anne encouraged her. "Your time may come sooner than you think." ∎

MARGOT KEPT A DIARY, TOO

Anne's diary is well-known, but it turns out she wasn't the only person in the annex who wrote down their innermost thoughts, dreams and fears. Anne's older sister also detailed life in hiding—but unfortunately, what became of Margot's secret diary remains a mystery, as it wasn't found with the items recovered after the families were taken from the annex by the Nazis.

The only proof the diary existed can be found in Anne's own writings. On October 14, 1942, she recounted a late-night conversation with Margot. "She asked if she could read my diary once in a while. 'Parts of it,' I said, and asked about hers. She gave me permission to read her diary as well." Still, Anne never mentioned it again.

Although Margot's diary didn't survive the Holocaust, a number of authors have imagined what she may have written about in her own "Kitty." In *The Silent Sister*, Mazal-Alouf Mizrahi writes from the perspective of the sensitive and thoughtful Margot as she describes life in Amsterdam as a Jew during the occupation, hiding in the annex and, ultimately, the Nazi camps that led to her death in February 1945.

Had Margot's diary ever been discovered, her friend Jetteke Frijda believed she would not have wanted her words to be published like Anne's, as she was the opposite of her "extroverted" younger sister, noted Jetteke. "Margot would not have wanted her private thoughts exposed to the world."

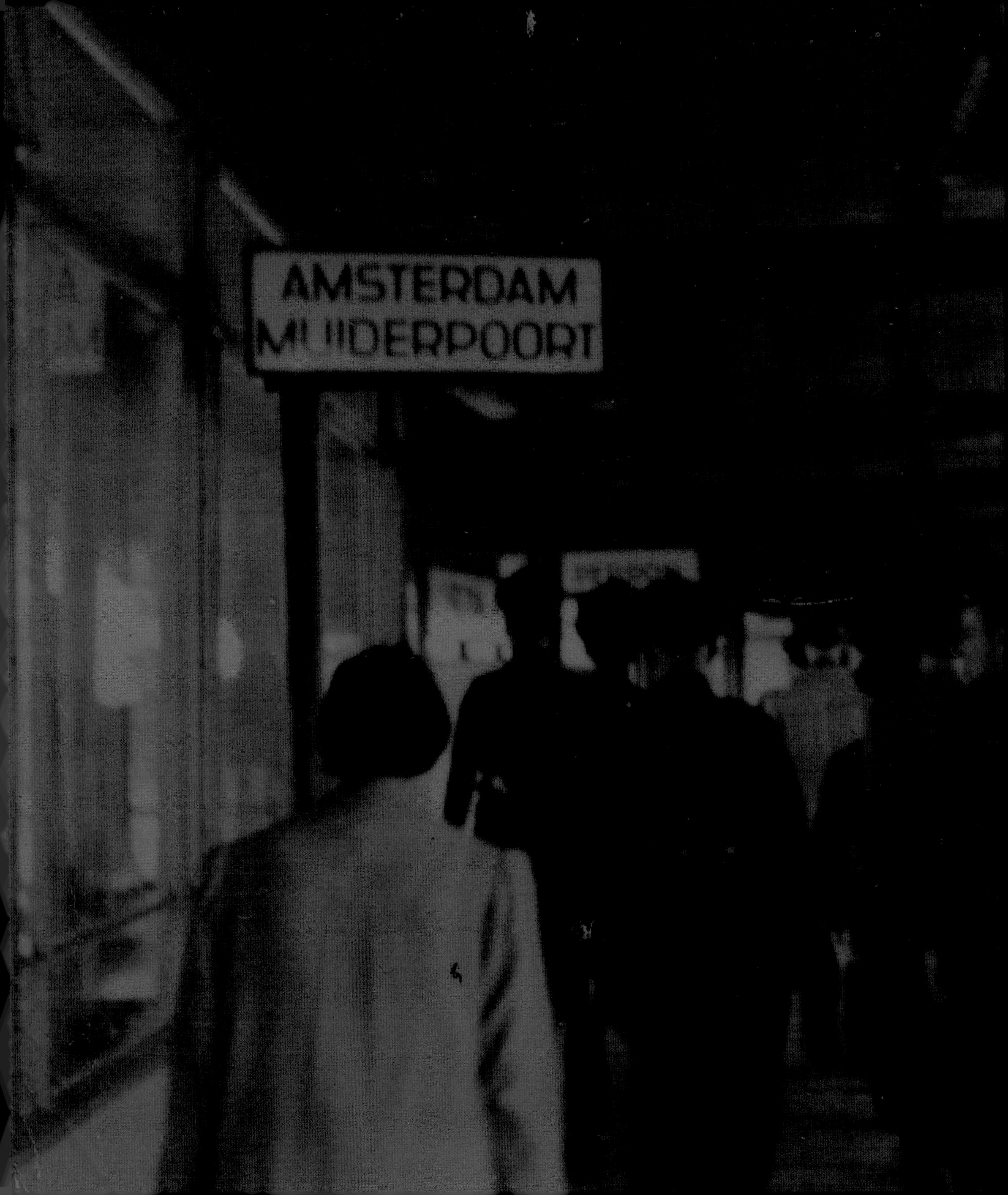
AMSTERDAM
MUIDERPOORT

FOUND OUT

Tipped off by an informer, the Gestapo raided the Secret Annex in August 1944. The Franks were arrested and sent to a series of increasingly horrific concentration camps.

2300

Karl Josef
Silberbauer
refused to
reveal who
tipped off
the Gestapo.

Discovered by the Nazis

As "Jew hunters" scoured Amsterdam for those in hiding, the Gestapo received an anonymous call that led them to the Secret Annex—and they arrested everyone inside.

Following the raid, everyone was sent to the Weteringschans detention center for three days.

After nearly two freedom seemed

ON JUNE 6, 1944, D-DAY, ALLIED TROOPS DESCENDED ON the shores of Normandy, France, on a mission to take back the country from Nazi Germany, then systematically free all occupied territories in Europe. Rescue couldn't come soon enough: Multiple raids throughout Amsterdam had resulted in the arrest and deportation of an estimated 17,000 Jews, but thousands more were still in hiding—and Adolf Hitler was intent on finding every last one of them. While Anne and her father remained optimistic, her sister and mother "were the most cautious in their estimates of just how long it would take for the Allies to liberate us," according to helper Miep Gies.

As they waited, fear grew in the Secret Annex. "Jew hunters" were being paid 40 guilders (Dutch currency) a head to do the Nazis' dirty work, and a number of frightening episodes at 263 Prinsengracht made it seem like they might soon be discovered. The closest came in early April 1944, when "I really thought I was going to die," revealed Anne, who detailed the incident in her

"I WAITED FOR THE POLICE AND I WAS READY FOR DEATH, LIKE A SOLDIER ON A BATTLEFIELD."
Anne, on the night the Secret Annex was nearly discovered

diary. That night, the group heard a suspicious noise down in the warehouse. The men—Otto Frank, Hermann and Peter van Pels, and Fritz Pfeffer—went to investigate, and inadvertently interrupted a burglary in progress. Although they successfully scared off the criminals, while fixing the door that had been kicked in, a man and woman suddenly appeared on the other side and shone a flashlight in their faces. As the men rushed back upstairs, a "pale and nervous" Otto warned, "We're expecting the police!"

For an hour, all eight fugitives huddled together in terror on the annex's second level. Suddenly, there was a second commotion below. But this time, it was footsteps—and they were getting closer: "The private office, the kitchen, on the staircase," Anne recounted. "All sounds of breathing stopped, eight hearts pounded. Footsteps on the stairs, then a rattling at the bookcase. This moment is indescribable. 'Now we're done for,' I said, and I had visions of all of us being dragged away by the Gestapo that very night. More rattling at the bookcase, twice. Then we heard a can fall, and the footsteps receded. We were out of danger, so far!"

As they anticipated the police's return, Anne and Margot were instructed to lie on the kitchen floor and try to sleep. "Margot and I were each given a pillow and a blanket. Margot lay down near the food cupboard, and I made my bed between the table legs." By 2:30 a.m., Anne finally

years in the annex, within reach.

'MARGOT WAS WEEPING SILENTLY'

Everyone was in a frightful shock when the Gestapo raided the annex with guns drawn. All eight fugitives stood speechless with their hands raised as officers ransacked their secret home looking for valuables. Inside Otto and Edith's room, they snatched his briefcase, which contained Anne's diary and other writings, and mercilessly dumped its contents onto the floor. At that sight, Margot couldn't hide her overwhelming fear. "The only sign of emotion was from Margot, who was silently weeping," revealed Victor Kugler, who was present in the annex. Although the 1988 TV film *The Attic* depicted Anne as screaming during the arrest, that was not the case, clarified Miep Gies: "Only Margot cried."

WHAT HAPPENED TO THE HELPERS?

The office staff in Otto Frank's company, Opekta, in 1941.

The Jews hiding in the annex weren't the only ones arrested in the raid. The Gestapo also apprehended Johannes Kleiman and Victor Kugler along with the Franks, van Pelses and Fritz Pfeffer. Although Miep Gies was suspected of aiding the eight fugitives, she was not taken into custody, but was interrogated by Gestapo agent Karl Josef Silberbauer, who threatened the 34-year-old that if she tried to leave town, "We'll get your husband." The fourth Opekta helper, Bep Voskuijl, 24, avoided any punishment, thanks to Kleiman's quick thinking: While the officers were preoccupied looking for the annex, he gave the young woman his wallet and told her to flee to a neighboring pharmacist for safety. (He begged Miep to run as well, but she was too scared to move.)

At SD (the Nazi intelligence agency) headquarters, Kleiman and Kugler were separated from the rest of the group and questioned by Nazi intelligence officers, but they refused to speak. In retaliation, both were hauled off to prison—without the chance to say goodbye to their Jewish friends—and transported to a camp outside of Amsterdam. Luckily for 48-year-old Kleiman, who suffered from stomach ulcers, he was released a week later due to his poor health, at the insistence of the Red Cross.

Kugler wasn't as fortunate, and was transferred to two more camps before ultimately being selected for a death march headed to Germany seven months later in March 1945. During the trek, an Allied plane shot at the Nazi-led pack, and in the chaos Kugler managed to escape. After a few days, the 44-year-old came upon a village, where he borrowed a bicycle and pedaled more than 50 miles home.

Following his release, Kleiman returned to work. Nine months later, after surviving the war, Otto Frank returned as well, and the two partners continued to run Opekta together—until 1953, when Otto moved to Switzerland and left Kleiman in charge of operations.

With the popularity of Anne's diary, visitors regularly showed up at 263 Prinsengracht hoping to see the annex, and Kleiman always obliged. He was also instrumental in establishing the Anne Frank House, but sadly died at age 63 while sitting at his desk—a year before the museum opened in 1960. As for Kugler, he immigrated to Toronto to work as an electrician, but remained in touch with his old colleagues. And when he retired, he too got involved with the Anne Frank House, giving lectures on the young girl he once delighted with copies of her favorite magazine, *Cinema & Theater*.

In 1973, at Otto's request, the helpers were recognized as Righteous Among the Nations, a high-level Israeli honor given to those who helped Jews during the Holocaust. Eight years later, Kugler died from Alzheimer's disease at the age of 81. When asked why he risked his own life for the people in the annex, his answer was simple: "They were my friends."

A replica of the Righteous Among the Nations award that was given by Israel to the helpers.

"WHEN THE POLICE FOUND THE HIDING PLACE, I MAINLY FELT A TREMENDOUS DISAPPOINTMENT THAT SO CLOSE TO THE END OF THE WAR MY FRIENDS WERE CAUGHT."

Miep Gies, in an interview with Scholastic's website in 1997

dozed off, but an hour later she was wide awake again. What if they were discovered? Her mind raced as different scenarios played out: "If they were good people, we'd be safe, and if they were Nazi sympathizers, we could try to bribe them!"

When D-Day happened two months later, though, everyone in the annex was filled with "fresh courage," revealed Anne. "I have the feeling that friends are on the way. Those terrible Germans have oppressed and threatened us for so long that the thought of friends and salvation means everything to us! Maybe, Margot says, I can even go back to school in September or October." The dream became even more promising on July 20 when a group of German military officers who felt Hitler was destroying the country in a senseless war conspired to assassinate him. During a meeting with the Nazi Führer, Claus von Stauffenberg placed a briefcase containing a bomb under the table. Right on cue as he left, it detonated, but Hitler suffered only minor injuries. Still, "I'm finally getting optimistic," said Anne. "This is the best proof we've had so far that many officers and generals are fed up with the war and would like to see Hitler sink into a bottomless pit."

But to Anne's heartbreak, it didn't happen soon enough to save her family. On the morning of August 4, Karl Josef Silberbauer, an officer with the Sicherheitsdienst (SD) Nazi intelligence agency, received an anonymous call: Jews were hiding at 263 Prinsengracht. As the Gestapo raced to the location, it was business as usual inside the unsuspecting Secret Annex. Everyone was up and preparing for another typical day. Miep stopped by to pick up their grocery list, an interaction they always looked forward to, especially Anne. "As usual, [she] had many questions to ask and urged me to talk a little. I promised that I'd come back and sit and we could have a real talk in the afternoon when I returned with the groceries. But conversation would have to wait until then. I went back to the office and got started with my work."

Moments later, Miep looked up from her desk in the office she shared with Johannes Kleiman and Bep Voskuijl. In the doorway stood an officer pointing a revolver at them. "I think the time has come," Kleiman whispered. Another group led by Silberbauer stormed Victor Kugler's office. "Who's the boss here?" he demanded. When Kugler replied he was, Silberbauer ordered him to lead them to Opekta's storerooms, where he was made to open every crate. "I said to myself: If it is only a house search, I hope it will soon be over," Kugler recalled. But it was much more than that. "You have Jews hidden in this building," accused one of the officers. "Where are they?"

Although Kugler insisted he knew nothing, the Gestapo continued their inspection of the building—ultimately ending at the bookcase that concealed the Secret Annex's door. "My heart was pounding," described Kugler. "The three Dutch policemen were already busy trying to open the bookcase. The moment I had feared for years had arrived. One of the police officers pointed his gun at me and ordered me to go first. The others followed behind, also with their pistols drawn."

When he reached the top of the stairs, the first person Kugler saw was Edith Frank. "Gestapo," he whispered. "She sat quite still and in some state of shock." Another officer stormed into Anne's room, where she and Margot were reading, and ordered them to stand next to their mother. More henchmen rounded up Otto Frank and Peter van Pels, who were studying in the boy's room, his parents, Hermann and Auguste, and lastly,

Nearly 100,000 Dutch Jews were held at Westerbork prior to deportation.

This photo was taken on June 20, 1943, when Nazis rounded up Jews during a major raid in Amsterdam.

As punishment for helping Jews, Victor Kugler was held in a crowded cell with death row inmates.

Fritz Pfeffer. After 761 days in hiding, they had finally been discovered.

Miep sat stunned in her office as she listened to the commotion above. Then, "I could hear the sound of our friends' feet," as they were marched down the narrow wooden staircase one by one. "I could tell from their footsteps that they were coming down like beaten dogs." Across the Prinsengracht canal, Miep's husband, Jan, who had planned to visit his Jewish friends for lunch, watched it all unfold: The eight prisoners, "each carrying a little something," were escorted to a windowless truck parked in front of the building. As the convoy passed within 2 feet of Jan, he couldn't bear the sight. "I turned my face away," he admitted to his wife.

What came next was Anne's worst fear: Westerbork, a transit camp surrounded by barbed wire, where Dutch Jews were detained until being shipped off to Nazi death camps, such as Auschwitz in Poland. "It must be terrible in Westerbork," Anne wrote in her diary in 1942. "The people get almost nothing to eat, much less to drink, as water is available only one hour a day, and there's only one toilet and sink for several thousand people."

On August 8, four days after the raid, Anne would soon see the horror for herself. That morning, as she and Margot were waiting to board the train at Central Station in Amsterdam, they caught the eye of Janny Brandes-Brilleslijper, who was on the same transport to Westerbork. "It struck me that the two girls were dressed in sporty clothes, with sweatsuits and backpacks," Janny recalled, "as if they were going on a winter vacation." Hours later, upon arrival at the camp, Anne and Margot were forced to turn over their trendy garments for dark-blue prison uniforms with red patches and wooden clogs that didn't properly fit their feet. After a physical exam and lice check, they were then assigned to the punishment block, barracks created for "criminal" Jews who did not voluntarily report for deportation.

At Westerbork, everyone had to earn their keep with manual labor: For 10 hours a day, beginning

"AREN'T YOU ASHAMED THAT YOU ARE HELPING JEWISH GARBAGE? WHAT SHALL I DO WITH YOU?"

Gestapo officer Karl Josef Silberbauer, to Miep Gies

at 5 a.m., Anne, Margot and Edith had to take apart batteries with a chisel to retrieve the toxic ammonium chloride paste inside. A filthy job, it was still better than working outside. The women, seated at long tables, also were able to engage in conversation. "There was talk, there was laughter," recalled Brandes-Brilleslijper, who worked with Margot and Anne. "You kept your sorrow to yourself."

Jewish prisoners were keenly aware that Westerbork wasn't their final destination—and where they'd end up next weighed on their minds constantly. Would liberation come first? It seemed possible. By August 25, after the Franks had been at the camp for two weeks, Allied troops had made tremendous progress in their campaign to topple the Nazis: American soldiers took over occupied Paris and were freeing sections of France, advancing toward Belgium and next would be the Netherlands.

The rumor going around Westerbork was that the Soviet Red Army was also nearing. But as the Franks waited in limbo, between possible salvation and certain death, the truth was they weren't close enough. On Saturday, September 2, the family was selected to board a train bound for an unknown camp the very next morning. Even though transports had always left on Tuesdays, now the Nazis were in a hurry to keep their Jewish prisoners out of the reach of the Allies—so a final convoy would depart two days ahead of schedule. The despair was overwhelming, remembered Brandes-Brilleslijper, "because there'd be little chance that we'd be alive for the liberation." ∎

3 4 5

Miep Gies, shown here in September 1936, was one of Opekta's first employees.

MIEP'S PLAN TO SAVE THEM

Miep Gies' loyalty to the Franks didn't end once they were discovered in hiding by the Nazis. The day after the raid, she called up Karl Josef Silberbauer, the SD officer in charge of the annex raid, and asked him if they could meet about "something very important." Silberbauer agreed and instructed her to come to his office that Monday, August 7, at 9 a.m.

That morning, Miep bravely went right up to Silberbauer's desk—but he was surrounded by other Nazi employees. "Any spoken words would have been audible throughout the room, so I just stood and didn't say a word," she said. "All I did was rub my thumb against the two fingers beside it, the index finger and the middle finger—the sign for money." Silberbauer knew what she meant. "Today, I can do nothing," he replied. "Come back tomorrow morning at 9 sharp."

When Miep returned the next day, she was relieved to see Silberbauer was alone, and she got right to the point. "How much money do you want to free the people you arrested the other day?" she asked. "I'm very sorry," he told her. "I can't do anything to help you. An order just came down. I can't deal as freely as I would like to." But Miep didn't believe him. "Go upstairs to my boss," Silberbauer insisted and gave her the room number. But when she knocked on the door, no one answered, so she opened it—and realized why: Several high-ranking Nazis were seated around a table listening to the BBC: The Nazi's last major offensive in Normandy was being halted by Allied troops. "Who is in charge?" interrupted Miep. An officer stood up and approached the intruder. "He looked at me as though I were a lump of garbage, turned, and slammed the door in my face."

Dejected, Miep made her way back down to Silberbauer's desk where he sat waiting. "I told you, didn't I?" he sneered. "Now leave here." Unfortunately, it didn't matter anyway; she was already too late. That day, the Franks, the van Pelses and Fritz Pfeffer had boarded a train bound for Westerbork transit camp, where they would stay before being moved again—to Auschwitz.

At the entrance
to Auschwitz,
the sign reads
*Arbeit Macht
Frei* (Work Sets
You Free).

Last Train to Auschwitz

After being sent to a temporary camp, the Franks were deported aboard what turned out to be the final transport to the ultimate Nazi death camp.

ANNE AND MARGOT AWOKE TO THE TERROR OF BARKING DOGS at dawn on September 3, 1944. The time had come to be transported from Westerbork to a new camp, and Nazi guards were ordering them to grab their belongings and line up at once. As the sun began to rise, the Frank sisters and their parents, Otto and Edith, marched along with 1,015 other Jewish prisoners to a nearby train station.

Where they were going, they didn't know, but how they would get there was apparent once they arrived at the tracks: windowless cattle cars. The inhumane transportation had haunted Anne as far back as October 1942, when she wrote in her diary about the "dismal and depressing news" that Jews were being hauled off in droves locked away inside cattle cars. "If it's that bad in Holland," she wondered, "what must it be like in those faraway and uncivilized places where the Germans are sending them?"

At Auschwitz, the four largest gas chambers could each hold 2,000 people at a time.

"EVERYTHING ABOUT OUR ARRIVAL IN AUSCHWITZ WAS SO UNREAL, SO BEYOND REALITY. IT LOOKED LIKE A SCIENCE-FICTION MOVIE."

Ronnie Goldstein-van Cleef,
who was on the Franks' transport

Anne would soon find out, but until then, it was going to be a treacherous journey. The Franks, along with the four others from the annex, were loaded into the cars, each packed to capacity with 70 people plus their belongings. With the doors bolted from the outside, they were effectively caged animals, and they acted like it: As there was not enough room to sit, the prisoners became aggressive and shoved each other for space. "The longer the trip lasted, the more belligerent people became," said Janny Brandes-Brilleslijper, who was in the same car as the Franks. "You get tired—so terribly tired—that you just want to lean against something or if possible, even if only for a minute, to sit down on the straw. Then you sit on the straw and they step on you from all sides because you are sitting so low. All those feet and all that noise around you makes you aggressive." Anne and Margot, noted Lenie de Jong-van Naarden, were protected as they slept leaning against their mother or father.

Inside the cramped cattle car, there was barely any light, just a candle in a can that hung from the ceiling. It was also stifling, as a tiny window covered with bars provided the only ventilation. In a corner sat a bucket for the dozens of men, women and children to relieve themselves, in front of each other without privacy. Within the first hour, it had filled—and spilled over, soaking everyone in human waste. "With 70 people it was a terrible mess," recalled de Jong-van Naarden. "During the trip, a couple of young men saw an opportunity to empty the pail through the crack between the doors. You can imagine how much it stank." Conditions were so horrific, people in a different car sawed a hole through the floor and dropped from the moving train. As it passed over them, it mangled one woman's hands and another man's arm—but they survived and were able to make it to a nearby village for help.

For two days and nights, it continued on like this, with no food or water. All the while, the Franks still didn't know where they were headed, only that they were aboard the very last transport out of Westerbork. Since July 1942, 100 "special trains" filled with Dutch Jews had departed the transit camp bound for Nazi concentration camps located throughout occupied Europe. "We were told that we would go to Wolffenbüttel" in Germany, remembered Brandes-Brilleslijper. "[But] we told each other that we'd never get that far since the Russians were practically in Berlin. To go that far into Germany would be impossible." That convinced the prisoners they weren't going as far east as Poland either. "Poland—to be going to Poland—that was our worst fear."

And it became all too real when the train finally arrived at its destination: Auschwitz, the largest and deadliest Nazi concentration camp, spanning 25 square miles in southern Poland. As the doors flew open, crude neon lights flooded the darkened cars, blinding the occupants inside. "Move, move!" was all they could hear, as guards wielding machine guns shouted at them. "Everybody out!" In Anne and Margot's car, the confused prisoners scurried, piling out on top of each other, along with those who had died during the grueling trek. Even though it was night, "Everyone knew immediately where we were," said Brandes-Brilleslijper. "It was so insane—that moment of realization, yes, this is an extermination camp. It was dreadful, yes."

From a loudspeaker above, an angry voice barked orders at them: Women to one side, men to the other. Children, the ill and anyone too weak to stand could take a seat on nearby trucks.

MARGOT'S SACRIFICE FOR ANNE

The conditions at Auschwitz were so appalling, it didn't take long for Anne's skin to become infested by lice, mites and bedbugs. Within weeks of arriving at the camp, she was covered head to toe in painful sores and rashes, and sent off to Krätzeblock, the scabies ward.

Since the Nazis feared the disease was infectious, the Krätzeblock was completely isolated from the rest of the barracks and surrounded by a high wall. While the wall blocked out the sunlight during the day, it couldn't prevent vermin from getting in at night—and they'd scamper all over the ill patients, whose petrified screams pierced the quiet darkness. There also wasn't any clothing allowed in the ward, so the sick slept two to a cot, nude, with only a thin blanket to share.

Krätzeblock was such a dreadful place, Margot volunteered to go with her sister—but before long, she too had scabies. "The Frank girls looked terrible, their hands and bodies covered with spots and sores," described Ronnie Goldstein-van Cleef, who was also in the ward. "They applied some salve, but there was not much that they could do. They were in a very bad way; pitiful—that's how I thought of them."

Margot and Anne mostly kept to themselves in Krätzeblock, but they perked up a little when it was time to eat, especially the pieces of bread and stolen potatoes their mother passed on to them through a hole she dug under the wall. "They became a bit more animated," said Goldstein-van Cleef, "and they shared the food and spoke a little."

As it was a sick ward, patients died all the time. Worse yet, decomposing corpses would lay there for days until someone came along to collect them—in the same carts used to empty the latrines. "I didn't want to see it at all, but I still had to look. I was compelled to look," admitted Goldstein-van Cleef. "The Frank girls saw it, too. And they experienced precisely what I experienced. They were just as afraid and nervous as I was, and they were apprehensive, just as all of us were. The emotional shock at the existence of something like that—they felt that as well."

"Don't get on," cautioned prisoners behind the gates. "You are healthy. Walk!" The weary travelers from Westerbork were confused. Many, too desperate for a moment of relief, ignored the warning and instantaneously sealed their fates: Because the very young, elderly and sickly were of no value to the Nazis, the trucks headed straight to Auschwitz's gas chambers for extermination. "Perhaps that's the quickest way to die," Anne once wrote in her diary.

The remaining Jews were forced into rows of five, as Nazi physicians, including the notorious Dr. Josef Mengele, looked them over. "He didn't say anything; he pointed," recalled Ronnie Goldstein-van Cleef. "To the right, that was us, the young, and in their eyes the healthiest people. The others, the older people and the children, went to the left. We didn't understand what was happening." Unbeknownst to Anne and Margot, this process was called "selection," and it would be the first of many times they'd be subjected to it at Auschwitz (see page 112 for more).

Of the 1,019 Jews on their transport, 549 of them were instructed to go left—which led them straight to immediate death in the gas chamber. For some reason, even though Anne was not yet 16 years old, she was allowed to follow the rest of her family to the right. But little did she or Margot know that sadly, it would be the last time they'd ever see their father. "The men had been separated from the women immediately," Otto later told Miep Gies. Otto, along with Hermann and Peter van Pels and Fritz Pfeffer, were marched for 2 miles to the main camp, Auschwitz I, while the women were sent to Auschwitz II-Birkenau.

But first, they would be "disinfected." Once the women lined up in alphabetical order, the

On average, 1,000 bodies were incinerated per day.

humiliating process began—and it took all night. One by one, they opened their mouths so gold teeth and fillings could be registered. All jewelry had to be handed over as well. Next, in a small office, female Polish prisoners sitting in rows awaited them. When it was Anne and Margot's turn, a needle was repeatedly jabbed into their left forearm, creating a crude tattoo of their serial number. Given the high mortality rate at camps, this made identifying dead bodies easier since inmates were often made to remove their clothing. For Anne, Margot and Edith, their numbers fell somewhere between A-25060 and A-25271.

Moving on to a large room, they were forced to remove all clothing. Standing naked and ashamed before the male guards, they had their heads shaved (as well as pubic hair) to prevent lice infestation. For Anne, this was especially upsetting as her hair had always been a source of pride. Disturbingly, the piles of shorn locks were not discarded—the Nazis sold them to German textile firms to be used in blankets, woven fabrics, even pipe insulation marketed as horsehair products.

Everyone was then herded to a shower room, where either scalding hot or freezing cold water poured down on them—a relief since they feared it might be gas. Once the faucets cut off, the shivering women were ordered outside, still nude, to be sprayed with a delousing powder, before finally receiving a flimsy striped uniform with which to cover themselves.

The Frank women, along with Auguste van Pels, were sent to Frauenblock (Women's Block) 29. A barn originally built for 52 horses, it now housed 1,000 females who slept 10 to a bunk, on their sides "lined up like spoons." There was no mattress or pillow, but some improvised by laying their head on their belongings. The first night, a woman made the mistake of stepping outside the barracks and was immediately shot by a guard in a tower. But she wasn't dead. Anne and Margot had to listen to her wounded groaning for hours. "We didn't know what we should do—go out there or not," recalled Goldstein-van Cleef. "But the others shouted, 'No,

THE LAST TIME EDITH SAW HER DAUGHTERS

The first few weeks at Auschwitz, the Frank women were inseparable. Edith was so desperate to keep her daughters safe, she would escort them everywhere, even to the latrine, because danger was always lurking. "You might walk in front of an SS man by accident, and your life would be over," said Lenie de Jong-van Naarden, who advised Edith to be overprotective of Anne and Margot. "They simply beat people to death."

That image must have been burned into the worried mother's mind because there was an incident in which a Nazi guard attacked Margot for some unknown reason—and Edith intervened. Her punishment: Never seeing either of her daughters again. Anne and Margot were transported to Bergen-Belsen concentration camp in Germany, leaving Edith behind at Auschwitz. Without them, said de Jong-van Naarden, "the mother was in total despair."

no you have to stay in bed; that's not allowed.' That woman lay there, dying, in a gruesome way.... Early in the morning she was dead, lying in front of the barracks, and we saw that."

Every night that followed was just as terrorizing: At all hours, they'd be jostled awake for roll calls. During these, Nazi guards commanded prisoners to stand in rows, at arm's distance apart so they could not lean on each other for support, as they conducted a lengthy head count. "When someone made a mistake or if their numbers didn't tally, then they would start all over again," recalled Brandes-Brilleslijper. "We stood there for hours. It isn't at all amazing that people who were sick

DR. MENGELE

During the Holocaust, thousands of Nazi camps were scattered across German-occupied Europe. None were as deadly as Auschwitz, however, where at least 1.1 million of the estimated 1.3 million people held there between 1941 and 1945 were killed.

The most widespread method of mass murder was gassing, in which hundreds of prisoners at a time walked into chambers disguised as showers. Once cyanide pellets were dropped into the vents, it was a gruesome death, and it was not swift: It could take up to 20 minutes, during which screams could be heard through the concrete walls. Once dead, the bodies were burned in the crematoria, which emitted a thick black smoke and foul odor, a looming omen to the other inmates.

Hundreds of thousands of young, elderly and sick Jews transported to Auschwitz were led directly to gas chambers before they even walked through the entrance. Those who made it past that lived in constant fear, as selections were random and frequent—and signaled by the appearance of the camp's angel of death, Dr. Josef Mengele. One by one, they would stand before him as he arbitrarily decided their fate. Selection didn't always mean the gas chamber. For some, it was a slow torture. One girl was ordered to kneel on stones at Lagerstrasse, Auschwitz's main street, with no food and a basin of water nearby she was not allowed to drink from. For days, the starving child was on display, as she repeatedly collapsed from weakness or a sadistic jab from a passing Nazi officer, until she died.

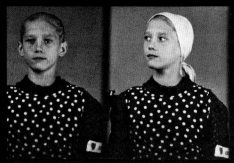

Although most young children were gassed upon arrival, some were spared and used for medical experiments.

Others were sent to Block 10, where Mengele subjected his "patients" to medical experiments, such as pressure-chamber testing, amputations without anesthesia, injections to change eye color and chemical sterilization. With a PhD in genetics, he was especially obsessed with studying twins and used them as guinea pigs to test X-rays, blood transfusions and surgeries, before killing them for the sake of an autopsy.

The depravity and death that permeated the camp was sensed by all living things, flora and fauna alike—and they stayed far away. "No fly flew there," described survivor Lenie de Jong-van Naarden. "Not a bird, of course, nothing. There was nothing, nothing that looked alive, no flower, nothing, absolutely nothing.... Auschwitz was really the end of everything."

"AUSCHWITZ IS NOT CALLED A DEATH CAMP FOR NOTHING."

Dr. Johann Kremer, Nazi physician in charge of mass gassings

dropped dead." Each day started in a similar fashion: At 4:30 a.m., guards returned to rouse inmates for another roll call, during which the most minor infraction, like a missing button, could result in a beating or even death. Margot and Anne often stood near Goldstein-van Cleef during this process, and she noticed the younger sister seemed withdrawn. "The fact that they had ended up there had affected her profoundly—that was obvious."

Twelve hours a day, they were forced into manual labor that continued until their weakened bodies gave out, what the Nazis called "annihilation by work." For Anne and Margot, that likely meant hauling stones from one end of the camp to the other, a repetitive, yet exhaustive task performed on little sleep and even less food. Breakfast consisted of only coffee—with five women sharing just one cup. In Anne's group, each took three sips and then passed it on. If there was enough left over, they'd be lucky enough to get a fourth sip. Lunch was a watery soup (meat and vegetables were added occasionally), and dinner was a piece of moldy bread with a tablespoon of cheese or marmalade and a tiny scrap of sausage.

Edith went to great lengths to feed her starving daughters. Once, she offered to trade her shoes for extra rations, but was betrayed and ended up barefoot. Another time, when a friend found a watch hidden in a mattress, Edith was able to sell it for a loaf of bread, cheese and sausage for Anne and Margot. Taking care of her children provided Mrs. Frank with a reason to go on at Auschwitz. "They gave each other a great deal of support," remembered survivor Bloeme Evers-Emden. "They were able to keep each other alive." But as Edith, Margot and Anne soon learned, it wouldn't stay that way for long. ∎

Bergen-Belsen
(here, after
liberation
in 1945) was
a wet and
filthy camp
crawling
with vermin.

Alone Together

With their parents hundreds of miles away, Anne and Margot were all each other had in their final months, as they suffered from starvation and disease.

At the height of the camp's typhus outbreak, 500 prisoners died each day.

Many prisoners were so starved, their stomachs couldn't digest solid food.

"WE DON'T HAVE ANYTHING AT ALL TO EAT HERE, ALMOST NOTHING, AND WE ARE COLD; WE DON'T HAVE ANY CLOTHES AND I'VE GOTTEN VERY THIN AND THEY SHAVED MY HAIR."

Anne, to Hanneli Goslar, once they were reunited at Bergen-Belsen

WHEN ANNE AND MARGOT ARRIVED AT AUSCHWITZ, THEY were accompanied by their mother and father. But just two months later, they left the killing center with only each other. On November 1, 1944, the sisters were sent to Bergen-Belsen in their native Germany to do forced labor in the country's war industry. It was considered to be one of the "better" Nazi camps, as there weren't any gas chambers. Instead, at six times its capacity, Bergen-Belsen was an overpopulated, "unorganized hell" with not enough food or shelter and ridden with deadly infectious diseases. According to Janny Brandes-Brilleslijper, who was on the same transport as Anne and Margot, they didn't know which camp they were headed to, but they believed it was better than where they were coming from. "As far as we could see, it couldn't get any worse. Nothing could be worse than Auschwitz."

Much like the journey from Westerbork, the prisoners were packed into cattle cars. This time, however, they were provided bread and water and were allowed to get out and stretch their legs during the multiple stops. When the train pulled into the station in the nearby town of Celle, "A lot of people said, 'Oh, we're going to Bergen-Belsen, now that's a good camp!'" recalled Janny, who was with her sister Rebekka. "But disillusionment followed immediately." It was pouring rain and hailing, yet the weary women were marched 4 miles, through the town and a forest, to the camp with only a blanket draped around their frail bodies. When they finally arrived at Bergen-Belsen, they were denied shelter from the winter storm: As there were more than 1,000 new inmates to process, the line to get into the main gate was endless—and they were expected to wait in it.

Freezing, Margot and Anne were huddled together under their blankets when they spotted two familiar faces: Janny and Rebekka. The Frank girls first met the Dutch sisters at Westerbork, where they spent hours each day talking while taking apart batteries. They were also on the same transport to Auschwitz, but assigned to separate barracks. Now at Bergen-Belsen, their reunion

LOST WITHOUT MARGOT

Throughout all the suffering that dimmed their young lives—religious persecution, hiding in the annex, starvation and torture, the loss of their mother—the Frank sisters always had each other. But when Margot succumbed to typhus, Anne, who wrongly believed their father was also dead, lost her only reason to go on living. "Margot had fallen out of bed onto the stone floor," recounted Janny Brandes-Brilleslijper, who cared for the girls. "She couldn't get up anymore. Anne died a day later. We had lost all sense of time. It is possible that Anne lived a day longer." While the time line is uncertain, Janny knew beyond a doubt: "She stayed on her feet until Margot died. Only then did she give in to her illness. Like so many others, as soon as you lose your courage...." But unbeknownst to Anne, she hadn't lost everything, and that's what haunted her friend Hanneli Goslar. "I always think, if Anne had known that her father was still alive, she might have had more strength to survive."

"WE PASSED THE LITTLE TOWN— THE PEOPLE SAW US, US POOR OUTCASTS. NO ONE LIFTED A FINGER TO HELP US."

Janny Brandes-Brilleslijper,
on the grueling march to Bergen-Belsen

was a great relief. "We thought, well, they've gone through the same things we have," Janny explained in the book *The Last Seven Months of Anne Frank*. "And then you are completely happy because you see that they've made it. At that moment there was only happiness. Only the happiness of seeing each other."

Once inside Bergen-Belsen, though, it was pure chaos. Camp officials weren't expecting the Auschwitz transport—and there was no room for them. In place of barracks, tents had been hastily erected, yet there still wasn't enough shelter for all the new prisoners. Desperate to get out of the cold rain, everyone ran to the tents, elbowing and shoving each other to get inside. "The Frank girls were bickering about whether they should go in," recalled Janny, "and then they did." That night,

a violent storm destroyed a number of the tents, including the one Margot and Anne were in, but the Nazis were in no rush to put them back up. As they shivered in the icy rain, according to Rebekka, Anne wailed, "Why do they want us to live like animals?"

Eventually, all four girls were relocated to the same wood-and-stone barracks, where the Brilleslijpers—who were a decade older than the Franks—acted as protective mother figures for their young friends. Once, a drunk guard stormed their barracks and tried to knock them from the top bunks. "He thrashed the sides of the beds with his whip," recounted Janny. "We resisted, tooth and nail, pressing ourselves against the bunks, and he couldn't get us.... We squatted on our upper bunk; above us was the sloped roof." There were moments of hope though, too. At Hanukkah, Anne and Margot celebrated by singing Yiddish songs with the other women and eating roasted potato peels, a feast to them. During the meal, everyone shared what they wanted to do once they returned home. When it was Anne's turn, she wished the Franks could enjoy a family meal at Dikker & Thys, one of Amsterdam's most expensive restaurants.

Without their parents at Bergen-Belsen, Margot and Anne had Auguste van Pels, yet she was no replacement for Edith, who, back at Auschwitz, was suffering greatly. Without her daughters, she had lost her will to live and eventually contracted scabies.

In the Krätzeblock (scabies block), Edith bonded with Rosa de Winter, who recalled the morning they were ordered outside for roll call. She and Edith had not slept the night before and were too tired to get up, but a Greek woman helped them drag themselves from their beds. As they stood in the yard, they watched guards empty out the scabies block, loading 300 ill women into trucks bound for gas chambers. Edith had cheated death, but only briefly. She soon developed a high fever and was sent to the infirmary, where she became so withdrawn, she stopped communicating. The last time de Winter saw her friend, "She was only a shadow. A few days later, she died, completely exhausted." It was January 6, 1945, 10 days before her 45th birthday.

To control typhus, prisoners were sprayed with poisonous DDT, a chemical pesticide.

At liberation,
13,000 unburied
corpses were
discovered at
Bergen-Belsen.

119

Under the supervision of American soldiers, German civilians were forced to bury the bodies of concentration camp inmates in April 1945.

Word of their mother's fate eventually made its way to Anne and Margot. They didn't know for sure about their father, but they assumed the worst. Around February 5, Hanneli Goslar, who had been Anne's friend since kindergarten, learned the Frank girls were also at Bergen-Belsen, but in a different section. That evening, she went to the barbed-wire fence that separated them—and caught the attention of Auguste. "I asked her, 'Could you call Anne?' She said, 'Yes, yes, wait a minute, I'll go to get Anne. I can't get Margot; she is very, very ill and is in bed.'" Yet when the 15-year-old appeared, "it wasn't the same Anne" Hanneli had known in Amsterdam. "She was a broken girl. I probably was, too, but it was so terrible. [Anne] immediately began to cry, and she told me, 'I don't have any parents anymore.'" (Anne was under the impression her father had been sent to the gas chamber upon arrival at Auschwitz.)

At Bergen-Belsen, Margot and Anne had also reconnected with Rachel van Amerongen-Frankfoorder, whom they'd met at Westerbork. But now, just a few months later, the bald and emaciated girls were unrecognizable: "They looked terrible," recalled van Amerongen-Frankfoorder. Amid the bleakness, there were brief glimpses of their former selves. Whenever Hanneli, who was being held in the "free" area of the camp, threw packages of food over the fence for Margot and Anne, "they would come back elated, very happy, and they would sit down and eat what they had gotten with great pleasure," said van Amerongen-Frankfoorder. "But you could see that they were very sick."

Because of the unsanitary conditions, prisoners were unable to keep themselves clean. And at the start of 1945, an outbreak of infectious diseases spread across the camp, with Margot and Anne contracting the most deadly one: typhus. They were sick with fever, muscle pain and rashes, but as the infirmary was overwhelmed, they had to remain in their barrack. Janny and Rebekka, who were nurses, did their best to care for the girls, yet every day they got weaker. "They had those hollowed-out faces, skin over bone," described van Amerongen-Frankfoorder. "They were terribly cold. They had the

"...AND THEIR END CAME. I DON'T KNOW WHICH ONE WAS CARRIED OUT EARLIER, ANNE OR MARGOT. SUDDENLY, I DIDN'T SEE THEM ANYMORE."
Rachel van Amerongen-Frankfoorder, on the sisters' deaths

least-desirable places in the barracks, below, near the door, which was constantly opened and closed. You heard them constantly screaming, 'Close the door, close the door,' and the voices became weaker every day. You could really see both of them dying."

The last time Janny saw Anne, she seemed to be in the final stages of the disease: apathy and confusion. Wrapped only in a blanket because she'd thrown her clothes away, "she didn't have any more tears." Three days later, Janny went to check on Margot and Anne, but their bunk was empty: The Frank sisters had become two of the 35,000 who perished from typhus at Bergen-Belsen. "The dead were always carried outside, laid down in front of the barracks, and when you were let out in the morning to go to the latrine, you had to walk past them," explained van Amerongen-Frankfoorder. "Then the heaps would be cleared away. A huge hole would be dug and they were thrown into it." (The camp was later burned to the ground to prevent further spread of the disease.)

The exact dates of Anne and Margot's deaths are unknown; it's believed to be either February or early March. Sadly for the sisters, they didn't survive to see British troops liberate Bergen-Belsen on April 14; the troops were met with the ghastly sight of 60,000 starving prisoners. And in January, their father had been freed from Auschwitz. Otto was weak and emaciated—and his only concern was for his daughters. When Eva Schloss, a friend of Anne's from Amsterdam, approached his bunk looking for her father, Otto begged: "Do you know where Anne and Margot are?" ∎

THE DEATH OF HITLER

Weeks after Anne and Margot perished, the Nazi leader committed suicide as the Allies closed in on him.

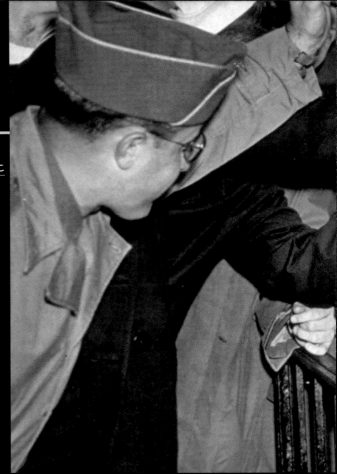

In Anne's diary, she closely followed the undoing of Adolf Hitler. Long before D-Day on June 6, 1944, a series of events signaled his empire was crumbling —and it gave her hope that freedom was near. In late 1942, Hitler's plan to seize the Suez Canal was thwarted by the Allies (led by the "Big Three," the United States, United Kingdom and Soviet Union), which blocked the Axis Powers (Germany, Italy and Japan) from advancing into the Middle East. Months later, Hitler's refusal to withdraw from the Battle of Stalingrad in Russia resulted in the complete obliteration of Germany's 6th Army, as well as the deaths of 200,000 Axis soldiers (another 235,000 were taken prisoner by the Soviet Red Army).

As Hitler's power weakened—and his biggest ally, Italian Prime Minister Benito Mussolini, was overthrown—the Allies leveled a crushing blow: Operation Overlord. Best known as D-Day, 160,000 soldiers landed on the shores of Normandy, France, from the air and sea, with the goal of liberating all Nazi-occupied territories in Europe and, ultimately, invading Germany, the country responsible for starting the war. By this time, in June 1944, it was clear to many high-ranking Nazi officials that defeat was inevitable—and they blamed Hitler for the certain demise of their beloved country.

Throughout the Führer's reign, he survived two dozen assassination plots, but none came as close as Operation Valkyrie on July 20. The failed attempt, by his own comrades no less, was the third in a matter of months. Now, Hitler's back was against the wall. "I'm finally getting optimistic," Anne raved the next day. To her, it hinted at the possibility of making peace with

the Allies—and ending the war. "But we haven't reached that point yet, and I'd hate to anticipate the glorious event."

Unfortunately, the annex was raided before she could see it happen. In late 1944, Western Allies (the U.S. and U.K.) and the Red Army advanced into Germany, dead-set on Berlin, home to Hitler. Until they reached him, the dictator did all he could to destroy what was left of his crumbling country before it fell into the hands of his opponents. But as he soon learned, he maintained very little authority. On March 19, 1945, Hitler instructed Albert Speer, minister of armaments and war production, to demolish all industrial infrastructures, but Speer did not. Similarly, on April 20, Hitler's 56th birthday, with the Red Army closing in on Berlin, he ordered General Felix Steiner's soldiers to fight back. They too refused to comply—and two days later, Soviet troops entered the capital city. Betrayed by his own commanders, Hitler declared,

In New York, U.S. soldiers celebrated the news on May 1, 1945.

New York World-Telegram

Hamburg Radio Announces

HITLER IS DEAD

EXTRA!

"Everything was lost," and informed his cabinet that he planned to remain in Berlin until the very end, when he would commit suicide to avoid being captured.

On April 28, Mussolini, who had inspired Hitler's own totalitarian rule, was caught trying to flee to Switzerland and executed, his corpse put on display at a gas station in Milan. That same day in Germany, Hitler learned Heinrich Himmler—his right-hand man who oversaw the establishment of concentration camps—had been secretly negotiating Germany's surrender. In retaliation, Hitler stripped Himmler of all power, expelled him from the Nazi party and ordered his arrest—in what turned out to be the dictator's last will and testament.

Hours later, just after midnight on April 29, Hitler married his longtime companion, Eva Braun, in a small ceremony at his bunker. The next day, with the Red Army just a block away, Hitler made good on his promise and shot himself in the head (Braun also killed herself by biting into a cyanide capsule). Even in death, Hitler refused to be in the custody of the Allies: His body, along with Braun's, was doused in gasoline and set on fire. When Soviet troops eventually discovered the charred remains, Hitler could only be identified by dental work on his lower jaw.

With its leader gone, the besieged country collapsed and officially surrendered on May 8, 1945—marking the extinction of Nazi Germany. It would be yet another three months before the third Axis power, Japan, also caved, finally bringing an end to World War II.

CHAPTER 5

SEARCHING FOR ANSWERS

In the aftermath of the Holocaust, Otto Frank tried to rebuild his shattered life. Despite all he had suffered, he never lost his faith in humanity.

"What Happened to Margot and Anne?"

Eva Schloss, Laureen Nussbaum and others recall Otto Frank's desperate search for his daughters— and the moment he learned of their deaths.

WHILE SEPARATED FROM HIS WIFE AND DAUGHTERS AT Auschwitz, not a moment went by that Otto Frank didn't think about them: How were they suffering? Were they starving or sick? Had they been sent to the gas chamber? When the concentration camp was finally liberated on January 27, 1945, he didn't immediately get an answer. Too weak to walk, Otto was lying in his bunk when a familiar face approached him: It was Eva Schloss, a friend of Anne's from Amsterdam who was searching for her father and brother. Although it had been three years since she last saw him, the young girl immediately recognized Mr. Frank, even though the tall man had withered away to 114 pounds.

MARGOT
FRANK
1926–1945
ANNE
FRANK
1929–1945

בר בנובה אדם

SPRÜCHE 10 27

A memorial stone for Anne and Margot now stands at the site of Bergen-Belsen.

Anne (center) with her father, Otto, and sister, Margot, circa 1931.

"WHERE EDITH AND THE CHILDREN ARE I DO NOT KNOW. I MERELY HEARD THAT THEY HAD BEEN TRANSPORTED TO GERMANY."

Otto Frank, in a letter to his mother

"He was thin and gaunt with hollow eyes, wrapped in a blanket," she recalled in her memoir, *After Auschwitz*. "He raised himself from the bunk as I approached. I said, 'I think I know you. I'm Eva, the little girl who used to play with Anne in Merwedeplein.'" Otto remembered her as well and nodded—perhaps she had news about his daughters. "Do you know where Anne and Margot are?" he asked Eva, with desperation in his voice. Unfortunately, she didn't. "I had to explain that I'd never seen anyone I knew from Amsterdam in the camp." Unbeknownst to both Otto and Eva, the Frank girls were not even in Poland anymore: They had been transported hundreds of miles away to Bergen-Belsen in northwest Germany, where they contracted typhus, the infectious disease that had taken over the camp, and by this time, they were mere weeks away from dying.

Once Otto regained his strength, he chose to return to Amsterdam, hoping he might reunite with his family there. Because World War II was still raging, he had to take a detour: From Odessa (in Ukraine), he boarded a transport ship heading west, first stopping in France, where he then took a train on to Belgium, and finally, to the Netherlands.

One of the hundreds of Jewish survivors traveling with Otto was Rosa de Winter, Edith's friend at Auschwitz, and during the voyage, she broke the news of his wife's tragic fate. He was crushed— but still hopeful Margot and Anne had survived. Coincidentally, on the same transport to Amsterdam was Eva and her mother, Elfriede. During a rest

Anne (left) and Margot with their mother, Edith, in Germany circa 1934, before the move to Amsterdam.

This studio portrait of Anne sitting on Margot's lap was taken in 1933.

stop they crossed paths again with the widower, and this time Eva shared her condolences for his loss of Edith. "Otto nodded but seemed too weary and sad to hold a conversation," she remembered. Throughout the remainder of the two-month trip, Eva saw him again once or twice, "but he looked withdrawn, his thoughts obviously far away."

On June 3, Otto finally arrived back in Amsterdam, and moved in with two people he trusted implicitly, annex helpers Miep and Jan Gies. The 55-year-old spent every waking moment desperately searching for his daughters: He contacted refugee agencies, placed newspaper ads, even wrote to liberated Bergen-Belsen prisoners, looking for any word on Margot and Anne. The worried father also visited local Holocaust survivors, including Elfriede, who was seeking her husband, Erich, and son, Heinz, as well.

Although they had met just two months earlier on the transport home, Otto had no recollection of the encounter. "I'm sorry, I don't remember," he told her, according to Eva. "I'm trying to find out what has happened to Margot and Anne." At home with Miep and Jan, Otto lived on pins and needles. "Every time there was a knock at the door or footfalls on the steps, all our hearts would stand still," Miep wrote in her book *Anne Frank Remembered*. "Anne's sixteenth birthday was coming on June 12. Perhaps, we hoped...but then the birthday came and went, and still no news."

As he waited, Otto checked in on Jewish friends and neighbors who still lived at the Merwedeplein. When he stopped by the Kleins' home, he was "happy to find our family intact, still in the apartment where he had last seen us three years earlier," remembers Hannelore (later, Laureen Nussbaum). According to her, everyone held out hope that since Margot and Anne had been at Bergen-Belsen, which didn't have gas chambers, they managed to survive. Like Otto, Laureen's boyfriend, Rudi Nussbaum, was also searching for his mother, Ella, whom he learned from the Red Cross had been found alive at the same camp— and the pair bonded over their own desperate

This image of Anne at age 15 was featured on a Dutch postage stamp issued in 1980.

searches. "Day after day Rudi and Otto Frank went to the Amsterdam Central train station to meet straggling survivors coming from the East," adds Laureen. "The two men held up photos of their missing loved ones."

In mid-July, Otto finally learned the truth about his daughters—and was utterly heartbroken. Likewise, Rudi received word that his starving mother had died just weeks after Bergen-Belsen was liberated. Before Otto could accept that Margot and Anne wouldn't be coming home, he needed to be certain it was true, so he paid a visit to Rebekka and Janny Brilleslijper, the sisters who had grown so close to the Frank girls in their final months of life. "He asked if I knew what had happened to his two daughters," recalled Janny. "I knew, but it was hard to get the words out of my mouth. He had already heard from the Red Cross, but he wanted to have it confirmed...and I had to tell him that his

children were no more." Although Otto was a man with tremendous self-control, understandably, revealed Janny, "He took it very hard."

The devastated father later returned to Eva's home to deliver the sad news about her friends. "At that moment it felt like the end of his life," she described. "We all cried bitterly, and after Otto had left that evening I curled up on [my mother's] lap and we held each other for a long time. 'At least we have each other, Evi,' [she] said, stroking my arm, 'That poor man has no one.'" ∎

"WHEN HE CAME TO TELL US HE HAD LOST HIS FAMILY, HE WAS 57 AND HE LOOKED LIKE A GHOST."

Eva Schloss, on Otto Frank

THE FATES OF THE OTHERS IN THE ANNEX

Of the 1,019 Jews on that final transport from Westerbork to Auschwitz, only 127 survived the Holocaust—and miraculously Otto Frank was one of them. Their chaotic arrival at the concentration camp in September 1944, was the last time all eight people who hid in the Secret Annex ever saw one another, as the men and women were immediately separated and confined to different blocks on the property.

Hermann van Pels, 46, was deemed fit for hard labor and made to do road construction, along with Otto Frank and Fritz Pfeffer, until he injured his finger in October and was ordered to stay in his bunk for three days. But before his sentence was up, Nazis did a clean sweep of the barrack and sent everyone to the gas chamber, including Hermann.

A month later, Pfeffer was transferred to Neuengamme camp, where he continued to do manual labor under appalling conditions. And after just a few weeks, the 55-year-old dentist died from a gastrointestinal infection on December 20.

At Auschwitz, Auguste van Pels remained with the Frank women and "formed a unit," according to fellow inmate Anita Mayer Roos. But it was broken two months later when Auguste, Margot and Anne were transported to Bergen-Belsen. In February 1945, around the time the girls succumbed to typhus, the 42-year-old was sent to another camp, Raguhn, a satellite of Buchenwald, where she stayed for just a few weeks before being relocated again to Theresienstadt. After that, it's unclear how Auguste met her fate. Annelore Beem-Daniel, who met her at Bergen-Belsen, claimed she died from typhus on the journey to Theresienstadt and that her body was removed from the cattle car and left behind, next to the train tracks. But another woman on the same transport, Rachel van Amerongen-Frankfoorder, tells a more harrowing tale: She testified to the Red Cross that Nazi soldiers threw Auguste, while alive, under the train and killed her, a claim never corroborated by another witness.

The youngest member of the van Pels family died within weeks of his mother. At Auschwitz, Peter

worked in the mail room and, because of his job, he was able to get extra food, which he always shared with the men from the annex. On January 16, 1945, he was selected for a 65-mile death march to Wodzisław in southern Poland, but before he left, he visited Anne's father, who was in the sick ward. "Otto Frank

On the tracks to Auschwitz, snow covers the personal effects of Jews, circa 1945.

had begged Peter to try to get into the infirmary himself, but Peter couldn't or wouldn't," according to helper Miep Gies.

Dressed only in thin clothing (and with nothing but snow to eat), Peter still survived the grueling, weeklong trek, which had been diverted to Mauthausen in Austria. But forced labor in the mines of the Melk satellite camp landed him in the infirmary, where the 18-year-old's body finally gave out. Although it's unclear exactly what day Peter died, camp records list May 5, which was the same day American troops liberated Mauthausen.

After the Nazis were defeated, Otto Frank went on to live another 35 years, finding happiness again with his second wife, Fritzi.

Otto Finds Love Again

Anne's father mended his broken heart with a woman who was also widowed by the Holocaust: Fritzi Geiringer, the mother of one of his daughter's friends.

AS OTTO FRANK PUT THE PIECES OF HIS LIFE BACK TOGETHER without his wife and children, he had someone special to help him: Elfriede "Fritzi" Geiringer. Like Otto, she was an Auschwitz survivor who had lost her spouse, as well as a child, in the Holocaust. The two first met years earlier when the Franks and Geiringers were neighbors at the Merwedeplein. In 1941, after Jews were forbidden from attending the same schools as Dutch children, Fritzi arranged for her daughter, Eva, to receive private tutoring at home, and she knocked on the Franks' door to invite Anne to join the lessons. The next year, their lives paralleled when both families went into hiding, where they remained until being discovered in mid-1944, ultimately ending up at Auschwitz. Following liberation, coincidentally, Otto, Fritzi and Eva all ended up on the same convoy back to Amsterdam—but when the teenager reintroduced her mother to Anne's father, he was understandably too devastated to engage in conversation.

A few days after arriving home, though, there was a knock on the Geiringers' door: It was Otto. Eva welcomed him in and led him to Fritzi "and they talked for a long time," Eva recounted in her memoir *After Auschwitz*. Throughout the rest of the summer in 1945, "Otto continued to visit us, for mutual support." And after Fritzi received confirmation that her husband, Erich, and son, Heinz, had not survived the concentration camp, the 17-years-older widower became her confidante, as the two quickly bonded over their shared heartbreak. That holiday season, in a letter Fritzi wrote to her mother, she revealed what she had learned from her friendship with Otto: "[Mr.] Frank says that when we are sad it is very egotistical. We feel sorry for ourselves because we are missing something so vital to us, but we can't help those that are missing because they can't feel pain anymore."

As Otto got closer to Fritzi, he played a greater role in her daughter's life. "When I came back from the war, I was full of hatred, not only for the Germans but the whole world," Eva explained to the *Atlanta Journal-Constitution* in 2019. "Otto had no hatred for anybody. He told me that if you hate people they won't know it, but you will become a miserable person." Later, when Eva struggled to return to normal life in Amsterdam, where she was haunted by memories of Pappy, as she called her father, and Heinz, Otto arranged for the young

In 1963, Otto and Fritzi (center) met Pope John XXIII at the Vatican, and gave him a copy of Anne's diary.

"MY MOTHER WOULD SET OFF FOR WORK EVERY DAY ON THE TRAM.... OTTO WOULD RIDE ALONGSIDE ON HIS BIKE. AT EACH STOP [SHE] CAME OUT ONTO THE PLATFORM AND THEY BLEW KISSES AT EACH OTHER."

Eva Schloss

woman to get out of town: first, to Paris with his youngest brother, Herbert; then to London to accompany him for a World Progressive Judaism conference. Following the trip, Otto went on to Switzerland to spend time with his family, and he invited Fritzi and her daughter to join him there.

Back in Amsterdam, 22-year-old Eva continued to agonize over staying in her hometown and what to do with her life. Once again, Otto came to her rescue. At his suggestion, she took up photography and she was allowed to use the same Leica he had once used to snap pictures of Edith, Margot and Anne. "That camera is quite a piece of history, and I treasure it," Eva later noted. "Otto could see that I was talented in my own way." He also helped the young woman get a job at an art studio in London, where she eventually fell in love with Zvi Schloss, a German-Jewish refugee and student who lived across the hall from her in her boardinghouse. Before long, he proposed, but Eva politely declined. "Thank you very much," she replied to Zvi, "but I can't marry you. My mother is a widow and I want to be near her in Amsterdam."

When Otto and Fritzi heard this, they decided she should know the true nature of their relationship, after nearly seven years. "You may have noticed that your mother and I have been getting closer," Otto nervously told Eva while he was in London for business. "We've fallen in love and, once you've settled down, we've decided to get married ourselves." Although she was taken by surprise, it was clear "he was deeply attached to my mother—and it turned out their relationship was based on far more than companionship and mutual understanding: It really was a romance."

Now free to lead her own life, Eva accepted Zvi's proposal and they were wed on July 19, 1952, surrounded by her mother, Otto and a few friends. Yet when the elder lovebirds said "I do" the following year, they kept it a secret—but Eva understood once she learned their wedding date. "They married on November 10, 1953, the day before my father's birthday and Mutti [Fritzi's nickname] knew how much that would upset me."

Although Eva found Otto to be a wonderful stepfather and she was happy to see her mother so in love, she was only human after all, and she worried he'd take the place of her beloved Pappy. But Fritzi reassured her, explaining they were two different men for two different times in her life. Erich, she explained to Eva, was the perfect husband for her younger self: "He was dashing and exciting, and he made all the decisions for us." On the other hand, with Otto, it was an equal partnership—and one that enriched them both. "He really became happy again," noted Hanneli "Lies" Goslar, a friend of Anne's who remained close with Otto after the war. "I don't believe that he was a broken man later."

Indeed, Fritzi revitalized Otto. In a letter to a young woman who had read Anne's diary, he revealed he wasn't the same person Anne described. "All you know about me has happened twenty-six years ago and, though this period was an important part of my life, leaving unforgettable marks on my soul, I had to go on, living a new life," wrote Otto. "Think of me not only as Anne's father as you know me from the book and play, but also as a man enjoying a new family life and loving his grandchildren." ∎

LAUREEN'S BEST MAN

As Otto Frank found love again, he was able to share that joy with others. After returning to Amsterdam, he grew close to Margot and Anne's friend Hannelore Klein (aka Laureen) and her boyfriend, Rudi Nussbaum, and when the young couple decided to marry on October 15, 1947, Mr. Frank served as their best man. It was a no-frills affair: Just eight people gathered at Amsterdam City Hall to witness the bride and groom exchange their vows in a group ceremony with two other couples, officiated by a civil servant. "I said my vows as Rudi beamed," recalled Laureen, who wore a simple, knee-length white dress and carried a bouquet of multicolored dahlias. "My parents treated the 10 of us to a festive dinner at a restaurant called De Vijf Vliegen (The Five Flies), and that was the whole celebration." Otto's gift to the newlyweds was especially poignant: a four-volume anthology about the history of the Netherlands.

LIVING IN ANNE'S SHADOW

Despite being her stepsister, Eva worried people would accuse her of jumping on the "Anne Frank bandwagon."

It wasn't always easy for Eva Schloss to be known as "Anne Frank's stepsister," and it affected her relationship not only with Otto, but also with her own mother.

When Eva Schloss gained a stepfather in Otto Frank, along with the "very kind, wonderful man" came the shadow of the family he had tragically lost, especially his daughter Anne. As Anne's diary gained popularity all over the world, Otto fiercely dedicated himself to preserving her memory—and after he married Eva's mother, Fritzi Geiringer, that burden also consumed her, leaving Eva to feel abandoned, and understandably, resentful.

Following the Holocaust, Eva struggled with depression, and Otto did all he could for his stepdaughter. "He helped me in so many ways when I was feeling lost in my life, gently steering me in a new direction," she notes in her 2013 book, *After Auschwitz*. And although she greatly appreciated the support, since Otto talked so much about Anne, she couldn't help but wonder if deep down he wished that instead of dealing with Eva, it could have been Margot or Anne. "I often thought that he must mind that I was alive when his own daughters were not, but I can honestly say that he never conveyed that in all the time that I knew him. He treated me with all the care and attention that he would have done if I were his own flesh and blood."

Her mother, on the other hand, grew more distant as she and her new husband became inseparable, bonded by the burden of Anne and her diary. Fritzi always seemed to put Otto first, with her daughter a close second—even when she needed her most. In 1968, while pregnant with her fourth child, Eva suffered a miscarriage and was rushed to the hospital. With her husband, Zvi, away in Israel for several weeks, she was left all alone to deal with the loss of her unborn baby while caring for her three other children. "It was one of those moments when you want your mother," Eva recalls. But when she phoned Fritzi to tell her the sad news, she was busy dealing with Anne Frank business with Otto in Denmark. "It's just so difficult," Fritzi reasoned. "They have the schedule all planned...and what would Otto do if I wasn't here?" Although Fritzi did come three days later, Eva was upset—and jealous her deceased stepsister took precedence.

In the years after Otto's death in 1980, Eva inherited his labor of love, spreading Anne's message across the world. As with her stepfather, it's been an all-consuming responsibility. But over the three decades, it's also helped Eva step out from Anne's shadow. In 1988, after speaking so much about her own Holocaust experience, she was inspired to write *Eva's Story*.

Following its success, her mother suggested she then tell her brother's tragic tale. "Everyone remembers Anne," Fritzi told her daughter before she passed away in 1998, "but Heinz was a talented young man too—and his life was cut short. It's as if no one remembers it." During the Geiringers' two years in hiding, painting was a creative outlet for Heinz and their father, Erich, and when they were discovered, the boy stashed their works of art under the floorboards for safekeeping. On the train to Auschwitz, the brother and sister reunited and Heinz shared his secret with Eva, in case he didn't survive to recover them. Sadly, he didn't: The 17-year-old died of exhaustion after a forced march to Austria in April 1945. Months later, when Eva returned to Amsterdam, she found a treasure trove of 30 paintings, along with 200 poems written by her brother—and she recounted it all in 2006's *The Promise*.

As Eva created her own path, she was able to reconcile being eclipsed by another. "I was always introduced as Anne's stepsister. I thought, 'I have a name—and I survived,'" she told the *Mirror* in January 2020, before her 91st birthday. But now, she's at peace with the past. "I've a good life, a husband, children. How can I be jealous of someone who was killed before she was even 16?"

"ANNE WOULD HAVE DONE IT THIS WAY"

Through Eva Schloss' three daughters, Otto got to relive raising Margot and Anne. The loving grandfather taught the girls to ice-skate in Switzerland, bought them bikes to ride on vacation in Italy and entertained them with invented bedtime stories—but he was also so consumed with Anne it sometimes overshadowed their own relationship.

In Eva's book *After Auschwitz*, she reveals Otto wanted Caroline, Jacky and Sylvia to know all about his late daughter, even insisting they read her famous diary, "but sometimes they found this unnerving. Occasionally he would even call one of the girls 'Anne.'"

Otto also couldn't help sometimes comparing Eva's girls to his youngest daughter. "They wanted a grandfather, and whatever they did it was always, 'Anne would have done it this way,'" she revealed in an interview with *The Telegraph*, "and you know, they didn't know Anne, so there was always this ghost living with us, like a shadow." That eeriness followed them to Basel, Switzerland, whenever they visited Otto and their

grandmother Fritzi. Even though Anne had never been to the home when she was alive, young Sylvia would always beg her mother to sleep in bed with her "because she felt that it was haunted with a 'spooky' presence."

Although there was no doubt that Otto loved his granddaughters, Sylvia says she and her sisters were painfully aware they "took second place" to Anne, and there was "a barrier" that kept them from growing closer. "Maybe I was the one who put up that barrier," she admits, "but I felt that we always had to live up to his expectations of Anne."

UN SOL VED MYSTERY

A team of FBI and police investigators have been working hard to find an answer to the more than 75-year-old question— and are closing in on the truth.

Experts
are closer
than ever to
discovering
who really
turned in Anne
and her family.

141

ANNE
FRANK
HUIS

During Vincent Pankoke's FBI career, he went undercover as a Wall Street financier and investigated the cellphone communication of the September 11 hijackers.

ON THE MORNING OF AUGUST 4, 1944, KARL JOSEF Silberbauer, head of the Gestapo's Jewish Division, received a phone call from an informant about Jews hiding at 263 Prinsengracht. Within hours, his team had successfully raided the Secret Annex and arrested its eight occupants. Over the seven decades since, there have been plenty of theories, suspicions and investigations into who tipped off the Nazi intelligence agency about Anne Frank's family, yet no one has been able to uncover the truth. But today we're closer than ever. Cold Case Diary—which has an international team of 20-plus FBI and police detectives, criminologists, forensic scientists, profilers, historians and data scientists, led by retired FBI agent Vincent Pankoke—has been dedicated to solving the mystery, and the team is equipped with the most advanced technology to date.

Back in 1948, at the urging of Otto Frank, Dutch police carried out the first investigation into the betrayal, followed by a second in 1963 after Anne's diary received international acclaim, yet neither turned up any conclusive evidence (Opekta foreman Willem van Maaren was the main suspect; see page 147 for more). But: "There were huge gaps in the questions, leads that weren't followed up, many logical steps that weren't taken," Pankoke explained in an interview with Australian morning talk show *Today Extra*. "Not only that, but back then, they weren't able to utilize a lot of the modern investigative techniques that we have today."

Artificial intelligence—computers that mimic human cognitive functions, like problem solving—has been the greatest asset for Cold Case Diary: The group's investigation involves combing through millions of bits of information—a mammoth task that no single person would be able to complete in a lifetime. But with software developed by Xomnia, a "big data" company in Amsterdam, the overwhelming amount of evidence is processed by algorithms that draw connections and determine specific clues for the team to then follow up on.

And that's not all: The group's database, the first of its kind, also generated an interactive map of Amsterdam, noting the locations of all Nazi officers, collaborators, sympathizers and informants, as well as local raids of Jews in hiding, and their proximity to the annex. The benefits of such technology goes even beyond Anne's case. "Since we're casting such a wide net over the information, we've actually been able to solve a different betrayal," revealed Pankoke, "of another Jewish family that was arrested in the nearby area during about the same time period."

Before any of this could be achieved, the team first had to collect the information to be uploaded into the system. Beginning in 2017, they scoured millions of documents relevant to Anne's arrest, including recently declassified Nazi files, at archives in Germany, the Netherlands, England, Belgium, Israel and the U.S. (at the end of World War II, Allied countries took possession of Nazi records) and spent endless hours "translating, reading and decoding the bad writing." During one

of these missions in Washington, D.C., Pankoke hit the jackpot: a list of informants kept by the Gestapo in Amsterdam, as well as payment receipts for Dutch traitors, most notably Pieter Schaap, who received 10 guilders for betraying someone on Potgieterstraat, less than a mile from the annex.

With the preliminary research completed in March 2018, the team moved on to the investigative phase: looking into old clues and hundreds of new tips they received from the public. One source in particular claimed to currently live near 263 Prinsengracht and identified their neighbor as a onetime Nazi collaborator. According to Pankoke, who splits his time between the U.S. and Amsterdam, "The second and third generations out from World War II are more willing to talk about what happened, or what they've heard from their family members." Sure enough, by the end of that year, the team could enjoy the fruits of their labor. "What we do have is probably over 10 very solid leads," Pankoke revealed to *NBC News*, "good information coming in from relatives of victims and also relatives of suspects."

One of their informants might be surprising: helper Bep Voskuijl's son, Joop van Wijk. He revealed in his 2018 book, *Anne Frank: The Untold Story*, that his mother's younger sister Nelly was a Nazi collaborator and may have been the one who betrayed those hiding in the annex. The possibility was so strong, the team reached out to van Wijk and he was interviewed several times about his aunt Nelly, among others. His years of research—including firsthand accounts from family members—also interested Cold Case

"PART OF THE STORY IS BEING LOST TO THE SANDS OF TIME. IF WE ACCOMPLISH NOTHING ELSE—AND I'M CERTAIN WE WILL—WE ARE BRINGING ATTENTION TO THE ISSUE."

Vincent Pankoke, on the Cold Case Diary team

Diary and they utilized much of the information for their investigation.

Growing up, recalls van Wijk, "a recurring theme in my family after the war was the tension surrounding the matter of Nelly's contact with the [Germans]." Yet when he questioned the situation, "my parents carefully avoided the subject" or downplayed Nelly's Nazi link. But when he spoke to his mother's other sister, Diny, in 2012, "it turned out she had an entirely different version of the Nelly story. Diny didn't shy away from speaking the unvarnished truth about her sister during the war." Two years later, he met with Bep's former fiancé Bertus Hulsman. "He didn't hesitate to discuss any subject, like Diny," adds van Wijk, "and he too brought all kinds of bits and pieces of the puzzle."

Another person who provided important clues is a Dutch-born American named Edith Chutkow. During the Holocaust, her Jewish father was a professional photographer who documented the Nazi occupation and how it affected the lives of Jews, and several of his photo albums were recently donated to the United States Holocaust Memorial Museum. Chutkow's mother was a Gentile, which allowed her father to be sent to a work camp for Jewish men married to non-Jewish women, so Chutkow, who now lives in Williamsburg, Virginia, was able to avoid deportation. Because her family had lived a few blocks from the annex, "Pankoke was interested in what life was like on the outside during the time the Franks were hidden," she explained to

The Virginia Gazette. And during their five-hour discussion, "I was quite able to fill him in on that."

As an ode to Anne, Pankoke kept an online diary during the early days of his investigation and frequently provided updates on the case. In a March 2018, he teased an interview with a Holocaust survivor in the Washington, D.C., area who may have been Chutkow. "I hope to learn so much from her about what it was like and how she was protected and provided for," he wrote. "She could have been partly depending on the same network in the neighborhood of the annex. Besides that, for myself, I think this interview might give more insight into the peculiar situation prior to Anne's arrest."

Also while in Washington, D.C., Pankoke met with a male Holocaust survivor for a "really interesting conversation," he revealed in February 2018. The unnamed man not only provided him with a lead—but also microfilm he hoped would contain some clues. "It's a strange story though, if not fantastic," added Pankoke. "Did this person really interview a police officer in the '60s who was involved in the Anne Frank case?"

Throughout the Cold Case Diary's investigation, they've had the support of the Anne Frank House—and the benefit of their own knowledge. Gertjan Broek, the museum's historian who conducted his own two-year probe into the betrayal, has served as an adviser for the team. "Cold-case investigation implies reviewing 'the whole body of work' that [has been] done before," he explains. "Mr. Pankoke occasionally consults me about insights or opinions I have regarding old and new information." Although Broek's research suggested ration card fraud accidentally led to the annex raid (and not betrayal), he praises Cold Case Diary as "an interesting endeavor." Likewise, Anne Frank House executive director Ronald Leopold welcomes the perspective of a third party. "What is new about this one is that it looks at the case with forensic eyes. And we look forward to the results."

When that will be remains to be seen. When the investigation was first announced, Pankoke hoped

During WWII, Jews were given ration cards for foodstuffs, oil and fuel.

WAS IT JUST A FLUKE?

After all the theories, it's possible that in fact no one turned in the Franks to the Nazis. In 2016, the Anne Frank House published new research that suggested an investigation into ration card fraud, not a tip from an informant, led to the discovery of the annex. The idea is not so far-fetched. In a March 14, 1944, diary entry, Anne acknowledged the arrest of Martin Brouwer and Pieter Daatzelaar, Opekta salesmen who dealt in illegal ration cards. "B. and D. have been caught, so we have no coupons," she revealed. Three years earlier, the Special Unit of the Central Investigation Division was formed to investigate the illegal distribution of ration coupons—and often, their investigations inadvertently found Jews in hiding.

"While researching historical backgrounds of the diary, I found out about the arrests of the salesmen," explains Gertjan Broek, historian and researcher with the Anne Frank House. "It was clear pretty soon that very few facts are actually known and there is no solid evidence for actual betrayal. In order to clear this mystery—if possible at all—we need to broaden the perspective. The arrests of the salesmen, the coupon fraud and the 'cooking' of the books show that there was more going on in the building than hiding fugitive Jews. Incident reports and post-war statements also show the way hidden people could get caught in numerous ways, not just through betrayal.... I lean strongly to the possibility of coincidence, or more precisely: that the arresting officers did not know they would find the clandestine presence of eight Jews when they stepped into the building."

to close his case on August 4, 2019, to coincide with the 75th anniversary of Anne's arrest. Yet after HarperCollins acquired the rights to *Anne Frank: A Cold Case Diary*, the "landmark publication" was set for a summer 2020 release—but that has now been pushed back even further to 2021. After three-quarters of a century, they are in no rush. "There's no statute of limitations on the truth," says Pankoke. "This is a fact-finding investigation; we're not going to prosecute anybody. In fact, anybody that we're able to develop as a suspect has probably passed away by now. But I think we owe it to the victims and we owe it to all of the people during that time period who suffered through the Holocaust and lived. I think it will show that the world has a conscience." ■

JOSEPH "JOB" JANSEN

LENA VAN BLADEREN-HARTOG

WILLEM VAN MAAREN

NELLY VOSKUIJL

THE SUSPECTS

Who betrayed Anne and the occupants in the annex?
Learn about the primary people who have been
accused of snitching on them to the Nazis.

During the Holocaust, the bounty on the heads of Jewish fugitives was so high, it's no surprise that someone ratted out the people hiding in the Secret Annex. The Nazis had originally offered 7.50 guilders (approximately $55 in 2020) to the Dutch for information on any Jew who had violated orders to be deported to camps. But as Adolf Hitler's power began to weaken, they upped the ante and promised upward of 40 guilders per head.

Early on the morning of August 4, 1944, the day of the raid, Karl Josef Silberbauer, the head of the Gestapo's Jewish Division, received a phone call from an unknown informant that Jews were in hiding at 263 Prinsengracht. Within hours, his team had successfully raided the annex and arrested its eight occupants. Over the 75 years since the Franks, van Pelses and Fritz Pfeffer were discovered, at least 30 different people have been accused of betraying them to the Nazis. But who really did it—and why?

WILLEM VAN MAAREN
OPEKTA WAREHOUSE FOREMAN
No one has been under more scrutiny for being the betrayer than Willem van Maaren. Long before the raid, van Maaren was on everyone's radar because he showed great interest in what was inside the annex and repeatedly questioned if people were accessing 263 Prinsengracht after business hours. Anne first expressed concern about van Maaren in an August 5, 1943, diary entry: "The whole gang breathes a sigh of relief: Mr. van Maaren, the man with the shady past, and Mr. de Kok have gone home for lunch."

One morning in October 1943, when van Maaren arrived for work, he found a man's wallet in the warehouse and demanded Victor Kugler find out to whom it belonged. When the helper didn't—because Hermann van Pels had dropped it during one of his nightly jaunts downstairs from the annex—van Maaren took matters into his own hands and began setting up traps to prove his hunch. "He often placed a small stick of wood on the packing table with its end sticking out over the edge," Kugler recalled. "Because the space between the table and the containers on the other side was not very wide, it was very likely that someone passing through there would displace the stick." Van Maaren also spread flour on the floor, hoping to catch overnight footprints.

Despite van Maaren's snooping (and the fact that he was stealing from Opekta), Kugler felt it was too risky to fire him. Would he retaliate by telling the authorities about his suspicions? Coincidentally, on the day the annex was raided, van Maaren was the one police came to first, since the warehouse was on the ground floor, and he pointed them in the direction of the upstairs offices where the helpers worked.

After Otto Frank returned to Amsterdam from Auschwitz, he filed a formal complaint with the police to investigate van Maaren—which they did twice, in both 1948 and 1963. "With the arrival of van Maaren, the safe feeling we had until then about the people in hiding gradually disappeared," helper Johannes Kleiman told authorities in 1948. Still, during both of the investigations, there wasn't enough evidence to formally charge van Maaren with anything and he was exonerated. But although van Maaren maintained his innocence until his death in 1971, Otto reportedly told a Dutch newspaper years earlier, "We suspected him all along."

THE SUSPECTS

LENA VAN BLADEREN-HARTOG
OPEKTA CLEANING LADY

More than 40 years after the raid, a new name was thrown into the mix. In 1998, Anne Frank biographer and Austrian journalist Melissa Müller pointed the finger at Lena van Bladeren-Hartog, Opekta's cleaning lady and wife of warehouse worker Lammert Hartog—who also happened to be the assistant of Willem van Maaren. According to Müller, the foreman shared his suspicions with his underling, telling him that he had noticed unusually large amounts of bread and milk delivered to the building. Is it possible that Hartog then blabbed to his wife? After all, there were rumors the anonymous caller was a woman. And it's not likely van Bladeren-Hartog heard anything on her own. In a May 9, 1944, diary entry, Anne revealed "the new cleaning lady" was hard of hearing: "Very convenient, in view of all the noise that eight people in hiding are capable of making."

In Müller's own investigation, she learned that in July 1944, mere weeks before the raid on the annex, van Bladeren-Hartog asked Anna Genot, the wife of her boss at the Cimex cleaning firm, if she knew there were Jews hiding at 263 Prinsengracht. Around that same time, van Bladeren-Hartog also brought it up to helper Bep Voskuijl, who immediately went to her boss Victor Kugler with van Bladeren-Hartog's accusation—but it was too late to do anything. A week later, the Gestapo raided the building and arrested the eight Jewish fugitives. In a letter to Otto, Kugler later admitted, "We discussed whether we should find new quarters for you and the others because anything you hear on the street will soon be known all over town. The situation was becoming critical, and in the days that followed we talked about it often."

Although she wasn't named an official suspect, van Bladeren-Hartog was interrogated during the 1948 police investigation. She testified she was unaware that Jews were hiding in the annex until August 1944, when Hartog came home from work upset and told his wife about the raid. "Before that, my husband had mentioned that a baker was delivering large quantities of bread to the building," van Bladeren-Hartog claimed. "Whether the bread was intended for hidden Jews or not, we did not know. My husband and I never talked about that." For some reason, she failed to mention to police she had been Opekta's cleaning woman. In June 1963, a few months before the case was reopened for a second investigation, van Bladeren-Hartog died.

ANTON "TONNY" AHLERS
ANTI-SEMITIC CRIMINAL

In 2002, four years after Melissa Müller's assertion about Lena van Bladeren-Hartog, Otto Frank's biographer Carol Ann Lee named her own suspect: Anton "Tonny" Ahlers, an anti-Semitic thug who had previously blackmailed the Opekta owner. In April 1941, before the family went into hiding, the 23-year-old Dutch National Socialist showed up at Otto's office with disturbing news. "He said straight-out that he worked as a courier between the Dutch Nazis and the Gestapo, and he asked me for 20 guilders," Otto recalled in an interview in the late 1950s. "I gave him the money, and he gave me a letter. I opened it. It was a message from an acquaintance of mine to the Gestapo, saying I had expressed doubt about a German victory and had attempted to influence him." The man in question was Joseph "Job" Jansen, an Opekta colleague with whom Otto severed ties after he accused Otto of having an affair with his wife (read more about Jansen at right).

But Otto didn't appear to see Ahlers' actions as blackmail: He thought the young gang member who had been in and out of jail was doing him a favor by giving him a heads-up about Jansen. In fact, Otto credited Ahlers, who had betrayed other Jews in hiding, with saving his life and in a follow-up meeting, gave him another 15 to 20 guilders. Once in the annex, though, Lee believes, "Otto Frank was of no more use to him in that sense, so he betrayed them." After he returned from Auschwitz, he wrote a letter in support of jailed Ahlers to the Dutch Office for National Security, but they believed otherwise. "He was an informant for the German detective Kurt Döring, who worked for the so-called Amsterdam branch of the German security police and the SD," authorities wrote in a 1964 confidential report. "[Ahlers] has on his record convictions for theft, public violence and malicious property damage.... His behavior during the war bordered on punishable fraud."

Although it hasn't been proven Ahlers was the betrayer, his son Anton Ahlers Jr. told *Volkskrant* newspaper, "There's no doubt he did it," claiming his father received money from Otto until his death in 1980 (Ahlers died in 2000). But noted historian David Barnouw suggests the Ahlers family is simply seeking notoriety. "There's no smoking gun, and the theory has too many loose ends."

JOSEPH "JOB" JANSEN
ANTI-SEMITIC ENEMY OF OTTO

Anne Frank's father never would have been involved with a criminal like Tonny Ahlers if it wasn't for the betrayal of a man he once helped out. Joseph "Job" Jansen, his wife and his son had all once been employed by Opekta—she demonstrated how to use its products at trade shows and the men both did odd jobs around the warehouse—until the elder Jansen accused their boss of having an affair with his wife, Jetje Jansen-Bremer, in 1936.

But five years later, Jansen and Otto ran into each other on the street and "Jansen asked me, because I was a Jew, if I still received shipments from Germany, and I said yes," Otto later recalled. "Jansen said the war would soon be over, whereupon I replied that I was not convinced of that and that the Germans still had a lot of fighting ahead of them. Then we went our ways." But to Jansen (a known right-wing radical and an anti-Semite who later turned in two of his own sons to the Nazis for being anti-German), Otto's words were "statements hostile to Germany" and weeks later he intended to report him—until Ahlers somehow intercepted the letter.

ANTON "TONNY" AHLERS

MAARTEN KUIPER

ANS VAN DIJK

THE SUSPECTS

Could Jansen have reported his enemy to the Nazis? Although he clearly had a vendetta against Otto, the Jansens worked at Opekta's location previous to 263 Prinsengracht, so he likely would not have had any knowledge of the annex. Coincidentally, in the same month of the raid and arrests, Jansen was also taken into custody for theft. After his release in February 1945, he was detained again, this time by Canadians who had control of the area, and he was tried and convicted for six counts of "assisting the enemy in wartime," including writing the letter denouncing Otto to the Nazis. Of Jansen, Otto testified, "He is the one who does the real dirty work."

"If I were to stand before Mr. Frank, look him in the eye, and deny that I wrote that letter, he would surely believe me," Jansen said in his defense. "I am no anti-Semite, and I have always respected Mr. Frank and considered him a person of high standing." Still, Jansen was convicted on all six counts and sentenced to four years and six months in prison. In 1964, Ahlers revealed in a letter that Otto was convinced Jansen and his son had betrayed him. Two years later, Ahlers added, "the most likely warehouse worker/betrayer was Jansen Jr.," although he provided no evidence to support the claim.

NELLY VOSKUIJL
BEP VOSKUIJL'S SISTER

The most recent suspect to be named is Nelly Voskuijl, the younger sister of Bep, who was a helper and trusted Opekta employee. In a 2015 book co-authored by Bep's son Joop van Wijk, *Anne Frank: The Untold Story*, it was suggested Nelly, who ran away from her Dutch home at 17 to work at a German air base in France until 1944, could have been the informant. According to Diny Voskuijl, another sister, Nelly was angry at Bep for being sympathetic to Jews and turned over their whereabouts. The book, which also features an interview with Nelly's fiancé at the time, Bertus Hulsman, points to the fact Karl Silberbauer told investigators in 1963 the caller had "the voice

of a young woman," although in other interviews he intimated the caller had been male. According to van Wijk, Silberbauer was trying to protect Nelly "possibly because of shared Nazi sympathies—or because she knew too much about Silberbauer's past." Unrelated to the annex, the young woman was arrested and charged with collaborating with the Germans in October 1945. Despite that parallel, her sister Bep wasn't questioned during the investigations, "a grave oversight on the part of the police," Miep Gies later commented.

When Otto lost interest in the betrayer, many believed it was because he knew it was Nelly and was protecting Bep, who shunned public life, unlike the other helpers. Van Wijk also claims Otto removed mentions of Nelly's Nazi collaborations from Anne's published diary, possibly "out of loyalty for my mother." Whatever Bep knew, she kept it a secret until her death in 1983. Nelly died in 2001.

MAARTEN KUIPER
DUTCH POLICE OFFICER

While conducting research on Tonny Ahlers, Otto Frank's biographer Carol Ann Lee also discovered the criminal was friends with none other than Maarten Kuiper, one of the Dutch policemen who Otto, Victor Kugler and Johannes Kleiman identified as being involved in the raid (although Kuiper was never officially confirmed). "I think [Kuiper] actually made the call" to report the Franks, Lee explained. "I think he got the information from Ahlers. They were friends. Ahlers had so much information on Otto Frank. Maarten Kuiper was one of the major betrayers of Jews in hiding during that time." Indeed, he was known to be cruel, described as having "the penetrating gaze of a madman." And in 1948, Kuiper was executed for the murders of 17 resistance fighters and Jews, as well as his involvement in the deportation of several hundred more Jewish citizens. Despite his misdeeds, Kuiper was never officially suspected of being the annex's betrayer.

ANS VAN DIJK
NAZI SECRET AGENT

In 2010, Dutch journalist Sytze van der Zee pointed to Ans van Dijk, a Jewish woman who had been arrested and threatened with deportation in 1943 until she cut a deal with the Gestapo. To save herself, van Dijk became a secret agent and turned in as many as 700 Jews, including her own brother and his family, to the Nazis—leading to unsubstantiated speculation that she also ratted out those hiding in the annex. After the war ended, van Dijk was sentenced to death for her involvement in the capture of 145 people and executed in 1948.

Eight years after van Dijk's name was first brought up as the betrayer, a book supported that theory. Gerard Kremer, the son of a Dutch resistance member, revealed in 2018's *The Backyard of the Secret Annex* that his father overheard van Dijk talking about Prinsengracht, where the annex was located, while working as a caregiver in the same building as Dutch Nazi organization NSB in August 1944. Although it's possible the notorious wartime betrayer had mentioned Opekta's secret hiding place, there hasn't been a smoking gun confirming the notion.

The Anne Frank House, which carried out its own investigation in 2016, has shot down the probability of van Dijk's involvement. "We consider Gerard Kremer's book as a tribute to his parents, based on what he remembers and has heard," the museum said in a statement. "In 2016, the Anne Frank House carried out research into the arrest of the Frank family and the other four people in hiding in the secret annex. Ans van Dijk was included as a potential traitor in this study. We have not been able to find evidence for this theory, nor for other betrayal theories."

The view from 263 Prinsengracht shows the close proximity of its neighbors.

PRINSENGRACHT NEIGHBORS

Otto Frank later learned that many of the neighbors surrounding 263 Prinsengracht had their suspicions about what was really going on inside the building from 1942 to 1944. Some claimed to have heard the flushing of a toilet and voices long after Opekta's employees had gone home for the day. Others were convinced it was the Frank family—proving that virtually anyone could have overheard the speculation that they were hiding in the Opekta's unused annex.

CHAPTER 6

ANNE'S LEGACY

Anne's diary, which was retrieved by the
Dutch helpers after the raid and returned
to her father, has kept her memory alive
for decades after her death—in print,
on stage and on the big screen.

Diary Drama

When a childhood friend learned *The Diary of a Young Girl* had been heavily edited by Otto Frank, she spent decades advocating on Anne's behalf.

This copy of Anne's diary was displayed in Frankfurt, Germany— her birthplace.

Dit is Juni 1939.

Dat is de eenige foto van:
oma Hollander, aan
haar denk ik nog
zo vaak en ik wou
dat zij nog maar
de hemelsche vrede
bewaarde. Margot en

Dit is ook
in 1940,
nog eens
Margot en
ik. Het kwam
maar met de
kaalte dat Margot
de bovenstaande foto
1939 was nog niet erg
ontwikkeld was. Hij
was toen net als ik nu
pas en zelfs al ouder
heeft dus niet in dit geval
op mij meer te bijten. Anne Frank.
20 Sept 1942.

ik kwamen
haar wel
niet het we-
der en ik
weet nog it
het hof erg
laud, daar.
Dan heb ik mijn
haartjes om
gedaan, om
het er to
bij bij vor-
die alhoe...
Nu de ij
de ij als je
altijs heeft
Anne Frank.
20 Sept 42

"The Merry" was a triangle-shaped courtyard where Anne and Margot liked to play.

Amsterdam (Z), Panorama vanaf Wolkenkrabber

ANNE FRANK'S LIFE MAY HAVE BEEN CUT SHORT BY THE Holocaust, but her story will live on forever—even if a few minor details have been left out. When the annex was raided, the 15-year-old was in the middle of the painstaking process of rewriting two years' worth of diary entries. Five months earlier, she had heard on the radio about plans to produce a literary collection of personal journals and letters kept during the war, and she wanted her best work to be featured. "Just imagine how interesting it would be if I were to publish a novel about the Secret Annex," Anne mused. "The title alone would make people think it was a detective story." But before she could finish, that fantasy was interrupted when the Gestapo arrested everyone in hiding at 263 Prinsengracht.

Once the coast was clear, helpers Miep Gies and Bep Voskuijl sneaked back into the Franks' makeshift home to collect their belongings before Nazi officers returned. Inside Otto and Edith's room, Anne's writings were strewn all over the floor. "Amidst the chaos," Miep recalled, "my eye lit on the little red-orange, checkered, cloth-bound diary that Anne had received from her father on her 13th birthday." She grabbed it, as well as the loose pages of pink and blue papers containing revisions, and put everything in a drawer in her office for safekeeping, believing one day she'd give them back to the young girl—but she never got the chance.

Otto was the only annex resident who survived the Holocaust, and when he returned to Amsterdam, Miep presented him with the most precious gift. "I said, 'Here is your daughter Anne's legacy to you,'" she recalled in her book *Anne Frank Remembered*. "I could tell that he recognized the diary.... He touched it with the tips of his fingers. I pressed everything into his hands; then I left his office, closing the door quietly."

Otto had known that Anne kept a diary, as she had placed it in a briefcase beside his bed every night while they were in hiding. At the time, he promised her that he would never look at it, "and I never did," he insisted. But after the "miracle" that was Miep's discovery, he felt compelled to reconsider. For weeks, the heartbroken father tried to muster the emotional strength—and once he did, he couldn't put it down. "What I read in her book is so indescribably captivating that I just have to keep reading," Otto explained in a letter to his sister on September 26, 1945.

From that point on, he spent nearly every waking moment poring over his daughter's writings. "I was very much surprised about the deep thoughts Anne had," Otto revealed on the television program *The Eternal Light* in 1967. "Her seriousness, especially her self-criticism. It was quite a different Anne I had known as my daughter. She never really showed this kind of inner feeling."

The father was so proud, he shared the diary with anyone who would listen, including Anne's friends Laureen Nussbaum and Eva Schloss, as well as Eva's mother, Fritzi Geiringer. "He read slowly, but he was trembling," recalled Schloss, "and couldn't get far without breaking down in tears." For his family members who had immigrated to Switzerland during the war, Otto translated certain entries into German using Anne's typewriter and mailed them copies to read for themselves. And the reaction was always the same: The diary was "an important human document" and Otto should

LAUREEN NUSSBAUM

"IF WE STICK TO THE VERSION ANNE PLANNED FOR PUBLICATION, NOT THE HODGEPODGE THAT HAS EMERGED...THE DIARY IS EMINENTLY QUALIFIED TO BE DESCRIBED AS LITERATURE."

Laureen Nussbaum

QUESTIONS OF AUTHENTICITY

When Otto lost his family, Anne's diary was the only thing he had left—and for the remaining three decades of his life, it gave him a reason to carry on. Readers all over the world were so moved, they felt compelled to reach out to the father whom Anne so lovingly wrote about to seek guidance. "It was

his obsession, the reason for existence," said his stepdaughter, Eva Schloss. "If a father loses a child that is the worst thing, and it gave him a task."

Unfortunately, the success of *The Diary of a Young Girl* also brought out the worst in mankind, forcing Otto to fiercely protect his daughter's memory. First, there was the ongoing battle with American writer Meyer Levin for the rights of the story to be adapted for stage and screen, "which took their toll on Otto's fragile nerves," added Schloss. Although Levin's enthusiastic *New York Times* review of Anne's diary was largely responsible for the jump in book sales, Otto wasn't a fan of his script, as it was too somber. When a lighter version was eventually produced for Broadway, Levin took it out on Otto: He sued him—and in a nasty letter, even accused him of betraying his deceased daughter.

Then there were the Holocaust deniers who disputed the authenticity of Anne's diary. In 1959, Otto had to defend himself against two Germans, Lothar Stielau and Heinrich Buddeberg, who accused him of forging his daughter's words. It was only after a court ordered the writings be examined by experts—who deemed them genuine—that they finally dropped their baseless case. Still, in 1976, another anti-Semite, Robert Faurisson, reared his head and began distributing pamphlets claiming the diary was fake. Again, Otto went to court over the matter and won, and Faurisson was banned from further publishing.

Although it was proved over and over that Anne's diary was real, questions remained. As a result, another team of experts was sent to Switzerland to comb through every item in Otto's possession related to his famous daughter—but it would be over his dead body. Before the Germans arrived at his door, Otto, who was suffering from lung cancer, gave Anne's unpublished writings to his friend Cornelis Suijk for safekeeping. And for nearly two decades after Otto's 1980 death, those five pages remained hidden until Suijk sold them to the Dutch nation and they were eventually added to the official diary.

share it with the rest of the world. "At first, I was put off by the idea of publication," he said in 1968, "but I gradually realized that they were right."

Otto's desire to make the diary public did not outweigh his family's privacy, however. "There are too many things in it that nobody should read," he explained to his sister, such as Anne's harsh criticism of her parents' marriage. So, unbeknownst to almost anyone else, Otto combined his daughter's original entries (Version A) with the 215 pages of revisions (Version B) into one amalgamated and edited Version C—which was then released as *Het Achterhuis* (*The Secret Annex*) in the Netherlands in 1947. Five years later, an English edition, *The Diary of a Young Girl*, was published with an introduction written by former first lady Eleanor Roosevelt. A 1959 Hollywood adaptation starring Shelley Winters as Auguste van Pels, for which the actress earned an Academy Award, stoked even more interest in Anne's diary and it quickly became an international bestseller. In fact, when Laureen and Rudi Nussbaum visited Otto at his home in Basel, Switzerland, in 1969, he proudly showed his longtime friends bookshelves lined with copies translated into some 55 languages.

Back in America, where the Nussbaums had immigrated for a fresh start after the Holocaust, Laureen earned her doctorate from the University of Washington. The topic of her dissertation: female figures in the works of Bertolt Brecht, a left-leaning poet/playwright who had fled Nazi Germany the same year as the Franks. Shortly after defending her dissertation, Nussbaum shifted her attention to another writer with a similar backstory. "I wrote to Otto Frank to ask whether he had any objection to me examining the literary qualities of Anne's diary," the mother of three recalled in her 2019 memoir *Shedding Our Stars*. "He answered in December 1977 that, of course, that would be fine, but he failed to mention that Anne had rewritten her original diary and that two different versions existed." It wasn't until 1986, six years after Otto's death, that she finally learned the truth.

"THE WAY SHE TRIED TO MAKE EACH ENTRY A LITTLE JEWEL IN ITS OWN RIGHT IS ABSOLUTELY REMARKABLE."
Laureen Nussbaum

Why did he take the secret to his grave? "I have a hunch, but no knowledge," says Nussbaum, who lives in Seattle (her husband, Rudi, died in 2011). "I don't have it from him because he never let on when we talked about my studying the diary. He never let on that there was more than one version."

A scholar of German literature and a writer herself, she was "very upset" by Otto's decision to take liberties with Anne's words. "Nobody has the right to mess with anybody else's text, whether that anybody else is a child or not a child," Nussbaum told the *Jewish Telegraphic Agency*. "The author's last version is what people need to read. And so I have been on my soapbox for a quarter-century preaching the gospel of Anne's revised version." That rendition, she adds, exhibits the teen's evolution over the two years she kept the diary. "Anne had matured tremendously," praises Nussbaum, and she had the determination to rewrite all of her "childish" entries—which is why it was such a shame her hard work had not been fully recognized.

But Anne's dream didn't die with her. Nussbaum acted as a voice for her old friend, and after decades of tireless advocacy, she was finally victorious: In May 2019, the Secret Annex novel that Anne had in mind 75 years earlier was released as *Liebe Kitty* (*Dear Kitty*). While unfinished, "This is the book that Anne wanted to write and to publish," insists Nussbaum, who penned *Liebe Kitty*'s afterword and also traveled to Berlin to speak at its launch. "Anne's fragment was an epistolary novel, not just a diary. And it's remarkable. How a 14- or 15-year-old had the literary prowess and stamina to be writing with such an eye for what it takes to create literature is really amazing." ∎

IN ANY LANGUAGE

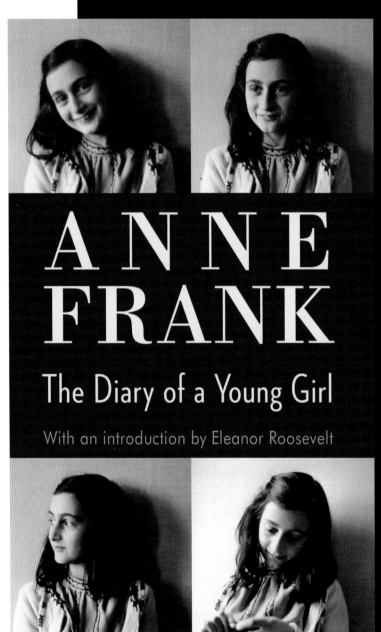

ANNE FRANK

The Diary of a Young Girl

With an introduction by Eleanor Roosevelt

The Diary of a Young Girl has been translated into 70 languages since its first Dutch publication in 1947. To date, more than 30 million copies have been sold.

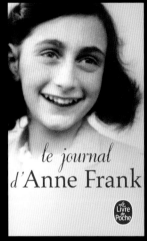

ANNE FRANK

Het Achter- huis

DAGBOEKBRIEVEN
VAN 14 JUNI 1942 - 1 AUGUSTUS 1944

The first title of Anne's book was *Het Achterhuis* (*The Secret Annex*), but after Doubleday printed the English language version as *The Diary of a Young Girl*, with an introduction by Eleanor Roosevelt, the book became a worldwide sensation.

ANA FRANK DIARIO

Anne Frank Tagebuch

Schatzinsel

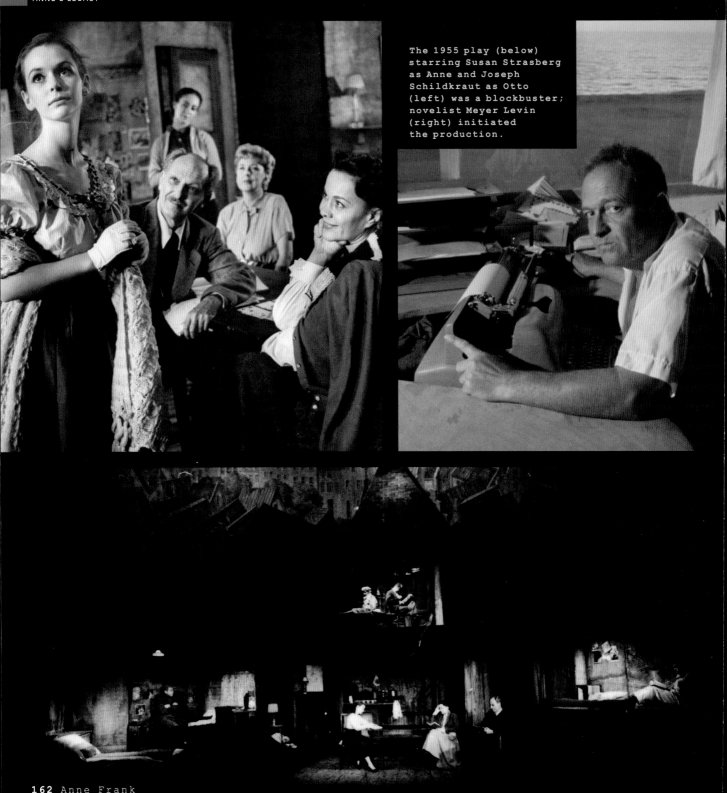

The 1955 play (below) starring Susan Strasberg as Anne and Joseph Schildkraut as Otto (left) was a blockbuster; novelist Meyer Levin (right) initiated the production.

Hollywood Ending

From Broadway to the big screen and beyond, dramatizations and documentaries help keep Anne's diary and legacy alive.

IT DIDN'T TAKE LONG FOR ANNE FRANK'S DIARY, ONCE IT WAS published in 1947, to gain worldwide notoriety— or for Hollywood to come calling on Otto Frank. From stage to screen and back again, Anne got her wish to "go on living even after my death," in the form of various actors portraying her, as well as numerous documentaries that have kept her legacy alive. Not all of the performances and adaptations have been created equal, but they have gone a long way—in concert with the diary itself—toward making the tragic teen writer a pop-culture star.

In 1950, American novelist Meyer Levin, who had covered concentration camps as a war correspondent in 1945, approached Anne's father with the idea of turning the diary—which had not yet been published in English—into a play or film. While Otto quietly agreed, the production became a litigious mess, with American publisher Doubleday bringing on two new scribes, husband-and-wife team Frances Goodrich and Albert Hackett, to write a play for Broadway.

The team jumped into action, corresponding with Otto about his expectations and traveling to Amsterdam to meet him and see the annex at 263 Prinsengracht. Their efforts resulted in the 1955 Broadway premiere of *Anne Frank: The Diary of a Young Girl*. The drama won a Pulitzer Prize, and with 18-year-old Susan Strasberg in the role of Anne, it earned four Tony Awards, including best play. Strasberg was nominated for her role, and strongly identified with her character. "She was only 10 years older than me," Strasberg said on NPR's *Fresh Air* in 1981. "We could have been friends.... There were nights before I went on stage when I felt she was around me."

The drama caught on and traveled all over the world: "This is the play that electrified audiences everywhere...and that—far more than the diary— invented the world's Anne Frank," wrote Cynthia Ozick in *The New Yorker*. Accordingly, the play was quickly adapted into a feature film in 1959, this time with Millie Perkins in the title role. Reading *Diary* "just hit me in my heart," Perkins once said. The movie, which also starred an Oscar-winning Shelley Winters as Mrs. van Daan (Anne's name for Auguste van Pels in her diary) and future *West Side Story* star Richard Beymer as Peter, won three Oscars, but it hasn't stood the test of time well. Even in 1959, *The New York Times* wrote that Perkins' Anne lacked a sense of the real girl's "spirit that will not die."

The 1959 movie, *The Diary of Anne Frank*, starred Millie Perkins and Schildkraut reprised his stage role as Otto Frank.

Still, both Hollywood and Broadway have continued to clamor for ways to bring Anne to dramatic life. Natalie Portman took the role in a rewritten stage version of the original Broadway play in 1997. Then 16, Portman said she did a lot of research for the role, including going to Amsterdam. "I met Miep [Gies] and Anne's cousin.... They showed me photos of her from a family album. It was heartbreaking because Anne is always smiling."

It's likely because Anne's smiling spirit still touches so many people that the documentaries and productions continue around the globe. In 2010, *Anne Frank Remembered* won an Oscar for Best Documentary, and the diary has even been turned into a musical—more than once! The Spanish-language *Anne Frank: A Song to Life* earned standing ovations in Madrid in 2008 and an off-Broadway production, *Anne Frank: The Musical*, had a sold-out New York debut in September 2019 (it closed in May 2020 amid the COVID-19 pandemic).

In early 2020, to mark what would have been Anne's 90th birthday, Oscar-winner Helen Mirren appeared in *#AnneFrank: Parallel Stories*, a big-screen documentary highlighting the famous teen's story, along with five other women who were also deported to death camps as young girls. "This is a story we must never forget," said Mirren. And 75 years after her death, it seems Hollywood and Broadway will continue to give Anne Frank a stage on which to shine. ∎

"SEEING A MOVIE LIKE *THE DIARY OF ANNE FRANK* OPENS PEOPLE'S HEARTS UP TO INSPIRE US TO MAKE OURSELVES KINDER THAN WE ARE."
Millie Perkins in 2009

ANNE'S CONNECTION TO AUDREY HEPBURN

Before she became a Hollywood star, Audrey Hepburn grew up on the other side of the world: German-occupied Holland during World War II. Although she wasn't Jewish, she did suffer at the hands of Nazis. Members of Hepburn's family were involved in the Dutch resistance and there were consequences for their actions: Her older half-brother Ian was deported to a Berlin labor camp and her beloved uncle Otto van Limburg Stirum was taken hostage and executed in 1942. Following the double tragedy, the future Oscar winner nearly starved to death during the Dutch famine, when Germans blocked resupply routes throughout the country. Years later, when Hepburn read Anne's published diary, she was devastated by one entry in particular. "I've marked where she wrote 'Five hostages shot today,'" the actress revealed. "That was the day my uncle was shot. And in this child's words, I was reading what was inside me and still there. This child who was locked up...had written a full report of everything I'd experienced and felt."

When the diary was turned into a movie in 1959, Otto Frank asked Hepburn to portray his daughter—but she was too traumatized by her own past. "I was so destroyed by it again, that I said I couldn't deal with it," Hepburn later admitted. "It's a little bit as if this had happened to my sister...in a way she was my soul sister."

Israeli President Shimon Peres reviews segments from Anne's diary during a 2013 visit to Amsterdam.

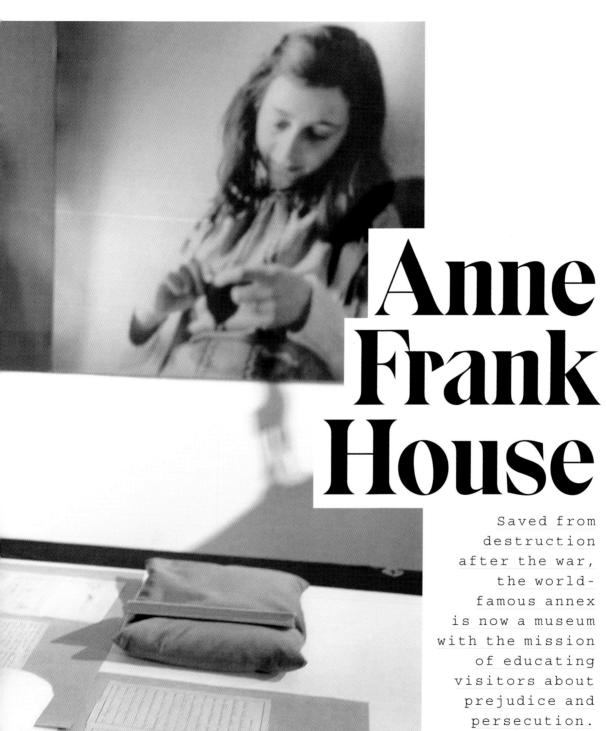

Anne Frank House

Saved from destruction after the war, the world-famous annex is now a museum with the mission of educating visitors about prejudice and persecution.

The Anne Frank House is one of the most popular places in Amsterdam, after the Van Gogh Museum.

IT WAS ANNE FRANK'S HOPE TO MAKE AN IMPACT, EVEN IF posthumously, that kept her going while she was hidden away from the rest of the world inside the Secret Annex. "I want to be useful or bring enjoyment to all people, even those I've never met," she wrote on April 5, 1944, just four months before her family was discovered and arrested. At the Anne Frank House in Amsterdam, she does just that. For 60 years, the museum has welcomed visitors from all over the world—young and old, regardless of their faith or skin color—continuing her message of acceptance and tolerance. In 2019, a record number 1.3 million people visited the place where the Jewish girl kept her famous diary during the Holocaust.

Following the wide release of *The Diary of a Young Girl* in 1952, fans and journalists began showing up at 263 Prinsengracht, all curious about the annex they had read so much about. Even though Otto Frank's spice company had moved to another location, Johannes Kleiman, who was one of the helpers, regularly returned to the empty building to give unofficial tours of the place made famous in Anne's book. By this time, however, the structure, which was originally built in 1635, had become so dilapidated, it was marked for demolition. Fearful of losing the remaining connection to his wife and daughters, Otto bought it in 1953, but could not afford proper renovations and reluctantly sold it the following year.

In the late 1950s, the building was once again threatened with being torn down. By then, though, Anne's memoir had spawned a Broadway

"I HOPE ANNE'S BOOK WILL HAVE AN EFFECT ON THE REST OF YOUR LIFE SO THAT…YOU WILL WORK FOR UNITY AND PEACE."
Otto Frank

Otto gave a tour of the annex for the CBS documentary series *The Twentieth Century* in July 1964.

It took 10 years to restore Anne's personal photos in her bedroom.

play and an Academy Award–winning film. Thanks to a campaign of prominent local citizens, the annex was spared indefinitely—and Otto seized the opportunity to turn it into a special place to honor Edith, Margot and Anne. In 1957, the Anne Frank Foundation was established and with the help of Amsterdam Mayor Gijs van Hall, 350,000 guilders was raised to renovate 263 Prinsengracht. "The spiritual value of the house is very great," Otto noted in 1959. "Thousands of people from all over the world have visited it the last years, many bringing flowers. And to be in the rooms where everything Anne wrote about had happened made an unforgettable impression on them. But more must be achieved. It is not enough that people are moved and come to think about all the terrible events. We must do more."

On May 3, 1960, Otto's dream finally came true when the Anne Frank House opened its doors. At the ceremony, he held back tears as he addressed the crowd. "I apologize for not speaking from this house after today," said Otto, who had moved to Switzerland by then (although he regularly returned to Amsterdam over the years). "You will understand that the memories of everything that happened here are too powerful. I can only thank you all for the interest you have shown in coming here." In the museum's first year, more than 9,000 people visited to learn about one of the Holocaust's most notable victims.

In 1963, Otto established the Anne Frank Fonds foundation in Basel, a nonprofit foundation (and the only legacy organization of the family) dedicated to the global distribution and licensing of Anne's diary, as well as an archive of thousands of photos, documents and personal belongings—the money from which all goes to education and charity. "It's quite impressive that somebody came back from Auschwitz as a survivor, having nothing left anymore, that he decided to create this foundation and put all his money, all income, whatever he gets from the diary, into the foundation," Yves Kugelmann, who sits on the Board of Trustees, says of Otto. "He said, 'This is

HOW THE ANNE FRANK HOUSE HONORS MARGOT

Visitors to the Anne Frank House in Amsterdam have the opportunity to learn more about Anne's older, often overlooked sister, Margot. Her life—from her early childhood in Germany and adolescent years to hiding in the annex—is illustrated using personal photographs, video interviews with friends and former classmates, quotes from her parents, and even letters she wrote to extended family.

In 2011, Margot was given the spotlight for the first time ever with the temporary exhibit "Anne's Sister." Permanently on display are a number of artifacts that provide better insight into the introverted sister Anne often complained about in her diary. The three years Margot spent as an only child are detailed in her baby book, in which Edith Frank recorded all of her first daughter's milestones, as well as gifts she received on her birthdays. There's also a diary once owned by her friend Jetteke Frijda, featuring a personal message penned by Margot.

For being so bookish, Margot was actually quite the athlete, and visitors can see a first-place medal she won for rowing, her swimming certificate and photographs of Margot playing tennis, skiing and ice-skating. In 2020, the Anne Frank House expanded its collection with two new snapshots of 15-year-old Margot rowing in the summer of 1941.

There are also mementos from her time spent in hiding. In 1943, Margot registered for a Latin correspondence course under the name of one of the helpers, Bep Voskuijl, and at the museum is one of the ambitious teen's graded papers, which Anne mentioned in her diary. "The teacher's very nice, and witty too," Anne wrote on November 17. "I bet he's glad to have such a smart student."

The museum has a portrait of Margot and her bicycle on display.

ANNE'S AMSTERDAM

Beyond the Anne Frank House, many of the places that shaped her life in the city are still intact today, from her elementary school to the Franks' first apartment building. Follow in her footsteps here—or, if you find yourself in Amsterdam, see it for yourself.

1 JEWISH CULTURAL QUARTER, CENTRAL AMSTERDAM The city's old Jewish neighborhood is made up of synagogues and memorials. At its center is the Jewish Cultural Quarter, about one-half square mile in the Waterlooplein and Plantage Middenlaan area; it includes the Portuguese Synagogue, National Holocaust Museum, Jewish Historical Museum and other important locations.

2 WATERLOOPLEIN FLEA MARKET, WATERLOOPLEIN 2 The oldest flea market in Amsterdam, it was a Jewish-run market until World War II. It's possible Otto may have stopped by on his way home to the family apartment on Merwedeplein Square before the Franks went into hiding.

3 JEWISH HISTORICAL MUSEUM, NIEUWE AMSTELSTRAAT 1 The museum moved to this spot on Jonas Daniël Meijerplein Square, where it's housed in four restored 17th- and 18th-century Ashkenazi synagogues across from the Portuguese Synagogue. The museum contains exhibits and presents events related to past and present Dutch Jewish life.

4 DE WAAG BUILDING, NIEUWMARKT 4 Built in 1488, this is the oldest building in Amsterdam and originally a gate in the historic city walls. Now the home of a technology and society research organization, the Jewish Historical museum opened here in 1932; Anne could have visited it before it was forced to close after the Nazi occupation of the Netherlands.

5 FORMER HOME OF JANNY BRANDES-BRILLESLIJPER, AMSTEL-101HS One of the last people to see Anne alive lived here in the Weesperbuurt en Plantage neighborhood, and it's where Otto received the news that Anne and Margot didn't survive the war.

6 HOLLANDSCHE SCHOUWBURG (DUTCH THEATER) PLANTAGE MIDDENLAAN 24 An ornate theater for the performing arts, this building entered a dark period when it was renamed the Jewish Theater and became the reporting point for an estimated 60,000 to 80,000 Dutch Jews, who were transported to the death camps. It now houses a memorial and educational exhibits. (The location will close for renovation in January 2021.)

7 THE NATIONAL HOLOCAUST MUSEUM, PLANTAGE MIDDENLAAN 27 Though closed for renovation until 2022, the museum is in a building formerly used as a teacher-training college and seminary. When it reopens,

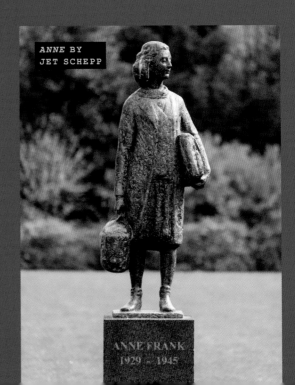

ANNE BY JET SCHEPP

ANNE FRANK
1929 – 1945

the museum will capture the story of the persecution and survival of the Jews in the Netherlands.

8 PORTUGUESE SYNAGOGUE, MR. VISSERPLEIN 3
Also known as the Snoge, this 17th-century building is still an active place of worship. It's also home to the Ets Haim Library, one of the oldest Jewish libraries in the world. The contents were shipped to Germany in the 1940s but returned to Amsterdam in 2000.

9 OPEKTA HEADQUARTERS, 263 PRINSENGRACHT
Now the location of the Anne Frank House (the entrance is around the corner), Otto's spice business moved twice before settling into this now-famous location.

10 ANNE FRANK HOUSE AND ANNEX, WESTERMARKT 20
When Otto returned from the war, he eventually bought the building, and in a few years he established

the Anne Frank House organization, which turned the into a memorial and museum that opened in 1960.

11 FORMER MARKET, ROSENGRACHT 13 Most recently a Tony & Guy hair salon, a market once stood on this spot where Miep Gies bought provisions for the Franks and others in hiding.

OTHER HIGHLIGHTS
- Childhood Home, Merwedeplein 37/ Merwedeplein Square
- Oasis Ice Cream Parlor, Geleenstraat 1
- Orthodox Synagogue, 63 Lekstraat
- 6th Montessori School, Niersstraat 41
- Jewish Lyceum, Stadstimmertuin 2
- Anne Frank Mural, Ms. van Riemsdijkweg 31

not my money. This is the money of my daughter and I would like to help make peace in the world.'"

To that end, the Anne Frank House expanded next door to 265 Prinsengracht in 1961 with the International Youth Center, where students from all across the globe can gather to take part in discussions, courses and cultural events centered around peace and tolerance. (In 2019, the Anne Frank House was also the site of more than 8,000 educational workshops.) By 1970, the number of daily guests—up to 1,500 in the summer months —was more than the museum could handle, requiring it to undergo a major renovation. Once completed, the Anne Frank House continued to grow, and in 1980, the same year Otto died, the annual number of patrons topped 336,000.

Despite its popularity, there was one vital artifact visitors didn't get to see for the museum's first 25 years: Anne's diary. When Otto moved away from Amsterdam in 1952, he took all of his daughter's writings with him. After his death, possession of the materials was transferred to the Dutch state, per his wishes. In 1986, the red-checkered diary Anne had received on her 13th birthday was finally put on display at the Anne Frank House. It was another 20 years before her two other journals— the 215 loose pages containing their revisions and a notebook of short stories she had written—made the collection complete in 2010.

Year after year, the Anne Frank House draws record crowds—half of whom are under the age of 30. Because of its many young visitors, the

GO WITH A GUIDE

If you prefer to walk in Anne's footsteps with a knowledgeable guide, there are several options for walking tours of Amsterdam. Most of them cover the Jewish Quarter highlights, along with other locations important to Jewish families like the Franks during the Nazi occupation. Some also include spots where the Dutch resistance tried to battle back against the German invasion and Nazi occupation. Be sure to check websites for the most up-to-date information available.

THE ANNE FRANK WALKING TOUR
This tour starts at the Jewish Historical Museum and stops by most of the important spots in the Jewish Quarter, ending at the Anne Frank House. (360amsterdamtours.com)

ANNE FRANK STORY AND NEIGHBORHOOD WALKING TOUR
This tour takes visitors through the South Amsterdam neighborhood of Anne's childhood, including the school she attended and where she played with friends, along with the house where Miep Gies lived for many years. (getyourguide.com)

LUXURY CANAL TOUR
Amsterdam is a city of canals, so it's not surprising to try a tour by boat. This one-hour trip starts at the Anne Frank House and heads along the many waterways. The guides provide an overview of Amsterdam history, including that of Anne and her family. (flagshipamsterdam.com)

PRIVATE TOURS
Several guides offer private Anne Frank tours around Amsterdam and many can be booked on TripAdvisor. Check out triggertours.com, which also offers tours of the red-light district and food tours that include samples of the cuisine, as well as day trips; or tomstraveltours.com, which features a variety of customized adventures led by locals.

museum has had to evolve: Ticket sales are now online only and its layout was redesigned to include historical context for those not as familiar with World War II. There was also an extensive two-year renewal project, which unveiled its first new exhibit in June 2018: a virtual reality tour of the furnished annex. Per Otto's request, the space has remained empty ever since the Nazis arrested its occupants and seized all their belongings. But now, with state-of-the-art technology, visitors can explore each room just as they were when Anne lived there. An audio tour was also added, which executive director Ronald Leopold explains, "gave us the ability to give information without disturbing what I think is one of the most powerful elements of this house: its emptiness."

For its 60th anniversary, the Anne Frank House truly was quiet. Amid the global coronavirus pandemic in 2020, it was forced to shut down for three months. During that time, however, those interested in her story could learn more on the museum's website, annefrank.org, and tour the annex virtually via its free app. On June 1, the Anne Frank House reopened just days ahead of what would have been its namesake's 91st birthday—but due to strict social distancing guidelines, at only 20 percent capacity. An independent museum that relies on admission revenue, the economic impact was severe and the Anne Frank House appealed to the public for financial support "if we are to continue to spread the memory of Anne Frank and her father's mission." ∎

On an industrial building in north Amsterdam, easily reachable by ferry from Amsterdam Central Station, you'll find a colorful portrait of Anne painted by Brazilian artist Eduardo Kobra (@Kobrastreetart) titled "Let Me Be Myself."

A statue of the
young writer
stands outside the
Anne Frank House
in Amsterdam.

Learn From the Past, Look to the Future

Her legacy is stronger—and more relevant—than ever: Anne and her family continue to inspire others as a new generation learns their story in a modern age.

Anne Frank *Video Diary* gives viewers an idea of what life in the annex was really like.

THE FURTHER THAT TIME MOVES AWAY FROM THE HOLOCAUST, will fewer people remember it? In the decades since Anne Frank's death, that has been a valid concern. But her legacy has proven more relevant than ever: As the coronavirus forced billions of people all over the world into isolation, obvious comparisons were drawn to her story. While the Anne Frank House acknowledges the "similar circumstances," it is quick to point out Anne's sole reason for going into hiding was because she was Jewish, and her persecution and death "were the result of deliberate human actions." Still, notes executive director Ronald Leopold, many of the same concerns plaguing youth during the global pandemic, such as not being able to see friends or go to school, "are bringing the story really, really close to readers in 2020."

Coincidentally, two years before the coronavirus pandemic, the Anne Frank House began working on "a new and appealing way of sharing Anne Frank's life story with young people." Yet when the project, *Anne Frank Video Diary*, was released as scheduled in March 2020, amid the crisis, it was a little too modern for some: The 15-part YouTube series reimagines Anne as a vlogger (video blogger). According to the museum, "What if, on 12 June 1942, Anne Frank had got a video camera as a birthday present, instead of a diary? Instead of writing diary letters, she would have made video recordings. The camera would have been her diary." To that end, readers are now viewers, an innovative format geared toward "young people who are less likely to pick up a book, but who do watch videos on social media."

Anne Frank Video Diary, which stars 13-year-old Dutch actress Luna Cruz Perez, focuses on the Franks' last five months in hiding, a time when

On what would have been Anne's 90th birthday, local students gathered at the Franks' Amsterdam home to hear from her friends Albert Gomes de Mesquita and Jacqueline van Maarsen.

Anne grew especially close to her older sister Margot (played by Shai Eschel). Each 10-minute episode features Anne talking to the camera about everything from her hope for liberation to her crush on Peter, as well as selfie-style "footage" shot from inside the annex. Despite the criticism, there is an educational framework: Seven episodes include a supplemental video that adds historical context and poses critical-thinking questions linking what Anne experienced to issues that exist in the present day, such as anti-Semitism and discrimination.

The unconventional project has the support of one of Anne's closest friends, Jacqueline van Maarsen. "By replacing the diary with a camera, young people can easily imagine themselves in that situation back then, when Anne Frank lived," says van Maarsen, who celebrated her 91st birthday in 2020. "The idea took some getting used to, but I think it's good that Anne Frank's story has been transferred to modern times." The project has resonated: Within weeks of its release, *Anne Frank Video Diary* racked up 1.5 million views—a reach that narrowly exceeds what the Anne Frank House achieves in a year. And after the coronavirus forced the museum to temporarily close in the spring of 2020, the digital series filled the void for those who couldn't visit in person.

More traditionally, Anne's story has been told on film (1959's *The Diary of Anne Frank* starring Shelley Winters), television (at least a half-dozen miniseries) and most universally, stage. In 1954, the first adaptation hit Broadway and was seen by more than a million people over its two-year run. Four decades later in 1997, the play was reworked, adding in newly discovered diary entries and starring Natalie Portman. On a smaller scale, "I'm told that every night when the sun goes down, somewhere in the world the curtain is going up on the stage play made from Anne's diary," helper Miep Gies once said (see page 162 for more).

In the 21st century, a number of new projects offered a fresh look at her life. In 2017, the Anne Frank Fonds foundation published the diary as a graphic novel by screenwriter and filmmaker Ari Folman and illustrator David Polonsky. Released

New books have a revisionist telling as to how Anne might have led her life.

in more than 20 languages, it was so popular, the duo reunited for an animated feature set for 2021. But *Where Is Anne Frank?* goes far beyond what is presented in the original material—it follows Kitty, the imaginary friend she wrote to in the diary, who wakes up in present-day Amsterdam determined to find out what happened to her owner. "We feel this adaptation shows a lot of the funny and brilliant sides of Anne's personality," explains Folman, who is also the Academy Award–nominated director of *Waltz With Bashir*. "Any new approach that will reach younger audiences

ENVISIONING ANNE AT 90

She didn't get to see her 16th birthday, but we know what Anne might look like if she were still alive today. In *Reflection*, a painting by Scottish artist Fiona Graham-Mackay, the young girl is shown in the annex's bathroom "looking to the future" in the mirror—and staring back is her 90-year-old self. Graham-Mackay, best known for her portraits of the British royal family, utilized computer technology to get a better idea of Anne's age progression, and the results are uncanny.

Graham-Mackay says the work holds special meaning for her. "*The Diary of Anne Frank* has been with me for most of my life," she notes. "I first read it when I was about the same age as Anne when she went into hiding. I was living in a very remote part of the jungle in Nigeria with my family, during the Biafran War. Books were scarce, and *The Diary of Anne Frank* was one of only four I had with me. It reflected a good deal of what was going on in my own life: the insecurities, restrictions, the fear of war and much I could identify with—and the real prospect of my own death."

Before creating the work, the artist visited the Anne Frank House in Amsterdam on a cold January morning, with a heavy downfall of snow in the forecast. The trees were stripped bare, and there were only a few people out, which led to the gloomy atmosphere. "I arrived at 8 a.m. to be shown around by the curator, before the museum was opened," she says. "Because we were the only people in the apartments where the family hid, I had a great sense of the space they inhabited and the life they led, a half-opened door leading into the next room, the view from the windows, the color—or lack of it. One thing that stood out for me was the bathroom where the occupants took turns to wash, including the sink and the tap handle that Anne's hand would have turned.

Mostly, the mirror caught my eye. What would Anne have seen when she looked at herself? What were her thoughts?"

Graham-Mackay was also intrigued by the cuttings and photographs taken from newspapers and magazines that Anne had stuck on the wall around her bed. "I could only guess what they meant to her, how she would lie in her bed and look at them, unsafe to look and join the world outside." Shortly afterward, the artist met Eva Schloss, Anne's stepsister who also celebrated her 90th birthday in what would have been the same year as Anne's. She spoke in great detail about Anne, her father and her own experiences during the war—and told Graham-Mackay that Anne would definitely have been a writer had she lived.

"The idea came to me that I would have the young Anne looking into the bathroom mirror and seeing her older self and the writer she would become," says Graham-Mackay, who added that she used the body of Schloss as the model for the elderly Anne. "Day after day, hour after hour, I worked on the face of the teenager, until youth gave way to adulthood, adulthood gave up its strength and ambition, and old age—with all its fear of not much longer to come—settled, with friends long gone and memories unclear. I then had the image of the 90-year-old Anne, as well as piles of folios on my studio floor of an aging, then aged heroine—the face of Anne today, had she survived. But she had survived by my pencil and brush."

The images seen pasted on the bathroom wall in the painting also hold significant symbolism, adds Graham-Mackay. A young Princess Elizabeth, pasted on the wall next to the sink, represents hope. "Every night, when possible, the family would listen to British radio," she explains. Above her is a bird in a cage, whose head points toward the mirror.

Reflection imagines Anne as she would look today.

"Restriction," she notes. "And freedom." To the left is a glamorous woman who is surrounded by two dashing young men, which Graham-Mackay says symbolizes Anne's own growing sexuality as well as the prospect of romance. And a picture of Aristotle on top is a nod to Anne's thirst for knowledge. "Anne had a natural instinct for learning and the family went to enormous lengths to keep themselves educated," adds Graham-Mackay.

Reflection was unveiled on June 12, 2019—Anne's 90th birthday—in London and was auctioned off to benefit the Anne Frank Trust U.K., which works to educate youth against all prejudices, regardless of race, gender or religion. It is now held in a private collection in central London. "I wanted the painting to reflect hope, even in the worst of circumstances," adds Graham-Mackay. "The future lies in educating our young."

EVA INHERITS OTTO'S MISSION

For the last half of his life, Anne's father was dedicated to preserving his youngest daughter's memory. And when he died in 1980, it didn't end with him: Otto's stepdaughter, Eva Schloss, picked up the torch, albeit reluctantly. Scarred by the loss of her father and brother and what she endured at Auschwitz, Schloss didn't even speak of the Holocaust until 1986, when she was invited to be on a panel at a traveling Anne Frank exhibit throughout England. "At first, it was a nightmare for me, as you can imagine," Schloss revealed in a 2019 interview. "I wasn't really a public speaker so it was really very hard. I always had to take a tranquilizer [beforehand]."

But the more she told her story, the easier it got —and she never looked back. Over the past three decades, Schloss has been dedicated to Holocaust education, recounting her story at more than 1,000 events all over the world, in addition to cofounding the Anne Frank Trust U.K. and publishing three books. "I have two lives," she said in 2013. "In one, I go out and travel the world and speak about Anne…. At home, I'm simply a housewife, a mother, a grandmother."

Even after turning 90 in 2019, she showed no sign of slowing down: Schloss made dozens of appearances all over the U.S.—including counseling a group of Newport Beach, California, teenagers involved in a viral Nazi-salute photo —as well as in the U.K.

And there's more to come. "There's plenty of work to do in schools," Schloss told the London Evening Standard. "There's always a new generation of people growing up who have to learn about the danger and the hatefulness of hating people who are different from yourself."

and readers is a blessing. We just hope it will inspire [people] to go back to the original diary and read it. It's a masterpiece."

That's the wish of the Anne Frank Fonds, too. The foundation, which Otto Frank founded, is highly selective with its projects. "We don't commercialize Anne Frank," explains board member Yves Kugelmann. And although Otto may not have been a fan of turning her treasured diary into a graphic novel, he would have seen the bigger picture. "At the end of the day, it was Otto who understood that we have to reach the next generation and it's our duty to do so without damaging the integrity of the book."

#Anne Frank: Parallel Stories also tells her story through the lens of others. Presented by Academy Award–winning actress Helen Mirren, the documentary intertwines the diarist's experiences with those of five other Jewish girls who were also sent to concentration camps, but who ultimately survived their ordeals. To give viewers a sense of the claustrophobia and oppression Anne faced while in hiding, Mirren reads from the diary in a perfect reconstruction of Anne's small bedroom in the annex. "I just feel *The Diary of Anne Frank* is an amazing teaching tool, an amazing vessel to carry the real understanding of human experiences of the past into our present and very much into our future," says Mirren.

More than seven decades later, Anne's story proves to be timeless—and there's a simple reason why. More than a book about the Holocaust, the diary is "about a growing teenager sharing a lot of problems she faced with her mother as a girl," notes Kugelmann. "It's a reality in each teenager's life." Indeed, the human component of Anne's diary is what continues to speak to young people, adds Ronald Leopold. "She's their peer. They recognize her voice, what she was thinking of, what she was doing when she was struggling with her relationship with her mother," he told Agence France-Presse in 2020. "That is exactly why it has remained relevant during the 75 years after the Second World War and why it will remain relevant, I am absolutely convinced, for generations to come." ∎

In 2018, diary pages Anne had covered were revealed to contain four dirty jokes.

A small statue
welcomes a new
generation of
visitors to the
Anne Frank House.

WHAT IF ANNE SURVIVED?

With the talent Anne possessed at such a young age, there's no question she would have gone on to find success as an author beyond her bestselling diary, according to those who knew her well.

"No doubt she would be encircled by children and grandchildren, as well as copies of published books and prizes won for writing them," helper Miep Gies once envisioned. "I believe she would have realized her wish to become a celebrated writer."

Childhood friend and scholar Laureen Nussbaum describes the diary as "literature," but also notes that Anne would have strived to be known beyond her famous work. "I know that she wanted to be 'the writer, Anne Frank' and to outlive herself as a writer rather than as a symbol," Nussbaum revealed in *Anne Frank Remembered*, the British documentary that earned an Academy Award in 1996. "Even more, however, she wanted to survive in person."

To Eva Schloss, Anne could have transcended inspiring others with her written word. "She might be in politics, she might be a social worker, she might be a writer—she would have had many options to choose [from]," Otto Frank's stepdaughter told the *London Evening Standard* in 2019. "On the other hand, her sister wanted to go to Israel. Perhaps she would have gone as well, perhaps she would have been disillusioned with Europe. It's very difficult to say."

A

After Auschwitz (Schloss), 126, 129, 139

Ahlerts, Anton "Tonny," 148–149

Amsterdam
  "Anne Frank" guided tours in, 174
  Frank family moves to, 24–35
  Jews deported from (July 1942), 75
  map of childhood locations, 172–173
  Nazis arrive in, 36–42

Anne Frank: A Cold Case Diary (Pankoke et al.), 145

Anne Frank: A Song to Life (musical), 164

Anne Frank: The Diary of a Young Girl
  (stage play), 7, 162, 163

Anne Frank: The Musical, 164

Anne Frank: The Untold Story
  (de Bruyn & van Wijk), 143, 150

#Anne Frank: Parallel Stories (documentary), 164, 183

Anne Frank Fonds foundation (Basel), 170, 179

Anne Frank Foundation (Amsterdam), 179

Anne Frank House, 99, 166–175

Anne Frank Remembered (documentary), 164, 185

Anne Frank Remembered (Gies), 66, 130, 157

Anne Frank Trust U.K., 181, 182

Anne Frank Video Diary, 177, 178–179

"Anne's Sister" (museum exhibit), 171

Attic, in secret annex, 76, 84, 85

The Attic (TV film), 97

Audio tour, secret annex, 175

Auschwitz concentration camp
  conditions in, 109, 111–113
  fate of Secret Annex occupants in, 132–133
  transport to, 106–107

B

The Backyard of the Secret Annex (Kremer), 151

Bathroom, Secret Annex, 75, 84, 85
  symbolism of images posted in, 180

Beauty ritual, of Anne, 81

Bedroom, of Anne, 78–79, 84, 85
  restoration of photographs in, 170

Bergen–Belsen concentration camp, Margot and Anne in, 114–121
  memorial stone, 127

Betrayal, of Secret Annex occupants, 140–145
  suspects in, 146–151

Boycott, of Jewish-owned businesses, 16

Brandes-Brilleslijper, Janny, 103, 108, 109, 111, 117, 131

Brilleslijper sisters, 117–118, 121, 131

Broek, Gertjan (historian), 144, 145

Brower, Martin (Opekta salesman), 145

Buddeberg, Heinrich, 158

Burglaries, at 263 Prinsengracht, 83, 96

C

Children, in Auschwitz, 112–113

Chutkow, Edith, 144

Cinema & Theater magazine, 52, 76

Cold Case Diary investigation, 142–145

Corpses, at Bergen-Belsen, 119
  burial of, 120

D

Daatzelaar, Pieter (Opekta salesman), 145

Dachau concentration camp, 16

de Jong-van Naarden, Lenie, 108, 111

de Winter, Rosa, 118, 129

Deportations, 29, 40, 42, 61, 75, 96, 103

Diary (Anne's), 6–7, 54–55, 78, 96
  early entries, 55–61
  jokes, censored by Anne, 183
  and other writings, displayed in Anne Frank House, 174
  pages censored by Anne, 183
  preserving memory of Anne, 153–161
  rewriting by Anne, as epistolary novel, 6, 78, 80, 156, 159
  unpublished pages, fate of, 158

The Diary of A Young Girl
  authenticity questioned, 158
  language translations, 159, 160–161
  Nussbaum on Otto's editing of, 159
  publication of, 158, 159, 169

The Diary of Anne Frank
    as graphic novel, 179
    movie, TV, and stage adaptations, 7, 169–168, 179
Dining area, Secret Annex, 74
"Disinfection" process, 110–111
Dressing up, 53
Dutch famine, 81, 165
Dutch resistance, 165, 174

E
Education
    on Holocaust, 178, 182
    on prejudice/persecution, 166–175
Enabling Act (1933), 16

F
Fashion sense, of Anne, 48, 49
Faurisson, Robert, 158
Folman, Ari (author), 179, 183
Food rations, while in hiding, 72, 76, 81
Frank, Annelies [Anne] Marie, 87
    death of, 117, 121
    diary of. *See* Diary (Anne's)
    early life of, 8–15
    legacy of, 152–185
    memorial stone, 126–127
    photos, 29, 31, 32, 33, 35, 128–131
    school years of, 46–51
    sibling rivalry and, 86–91
    statues of, 172, 176
    in Summer of 1941, 44–45, 171
Frank, Edith (née Holländer) (mother of Margot and Anne), 14, 129
    in Auschwitz, 111, 113, 118
    death of, 118
    Margot's closeness with, 33
Frank, Margot (sister of Anne), 15, 86
    behavior during arrest, 97
    death of, 117, 121
    deportation summons, 61
    diary of, 91
    honored in Anne Frank House, 171
    memorial stone, 126–127

    photos, 30, 33, 45, 128–130
    sibling rivalry and, 86–91
    in Summer of 1941, 44–45, 171
Frank, Otto (father of Anne and Margot), 14, 128, 169
    Anne's closeness with, 33, 83
    Anne's diary/writings returned to, 157
    in Auschwitz, 132
    as best man at Klein–Nussbaum wedding, 7, 137
    death of, 174
    learns of Edith's death, 128
    learns of Margot's and Anne's death, 131
    post-war move to Switzerland, 99, 170
    preserves privacy of family, 159
    publishes edited version of Anne's diary/ rewritings, 6, 154–159
    remarries, 134–139
    requests honors for the helpers, 99
    return to Amsterdam, 129–130
    search for his family, 124–131
    as step-grandfather, 139
Frank family
    attempt to flee to U.S., 43
    go into hiding, 61, 66–69. *See also* Secret Annex
    photos, 18–23, 33
Frijda, Jetteke, diary of, 171

G
Gas chambers, at Auschwitz, 108
Geiringer, Elfriede "Fritzi" (second wife of Otto), 130, 134–139
    surviving daughter. *See* Schloss, Eva (née Geiringer)
German economy, in 1930s, 16
Gestapo raid, on Secret Annex, 92–103
Gies, Jan (husband of Miep), 70, 73, 103, 130
Gies, Miep (employee/helper), 69–70, 73, 91, 104, 130, 183
    interactions with Silberbauer, 99, 105
    retrieves Anne's writings from Secret Annex, 6, 156–157

role in Frank family move to Secret Annex, 66, 69
Goldstein-van Cleef, Ronnie, 108, 109, 110, 113
Gomes de Mesquita, Albert, 178
Goodrich, Frances (playwright), 7, 163
Goslar, Hanneli "Lies," 29, 45, 49–50, 51, 55, 117, 121, 137
Graham-Mackay, Fiona (artist), 180–181

H
Hackett, Albert (playwright), 7, 163
Helpers, of Frank and van Pels families, 70–73
Hepburn, Audrey (actor), 165
Het Achterhuis (The Secret Annex), 6, 160–161
Hiding, going into. *See also* Secret Annex
    Miep Gies' role in, 66–69
    preparations for, 61, 68, 69, 70–71
Hitler, Adolf
    death of, 122–123
    resentment toward Jews, 16–17
    rise and reach of, 24–32, 35
    "subhumans" targeted by, 30
Hollywood
    Anne's legacy continued by, 162–165
    Anne's obsession with, 52, 79
Holocaust
    deaths during, estimated numbers, 30, 123
    diaries written by Jewish teenagers during, 6–77
    education on, 178, 182
Holocaust deniers, 158
Hulsman, Bertus, 144, 150

I
Incinerators, at Auschwitz, 110
International Youth Center (265 Prinsengracht), 174

J
Jansen, Joseph "Job," 146, 149–150
"Jew hunters," 95, 96
Jewish teenagers, diaries written by, 6–7
Jews
    deportations of, 29, 40, 42, 61, 75, 96, 103
    Hitler's resentment toward, 16–17
    restrictions on, 40, 41, 44–45, 52, 69

K
Kiss, first, 90–91
Kitty (imaginary friend), 55, 56, 78, 80, 179. *See also Liebe Kitty (Dear Kitty)*
Kleiman, Johannes (employee/helper), 70–73, 99, 169
Kleiman, Willy (brother of Johannes), 70–71
Klein, Hannelore. *See* Nussbaum, Laureen
Klein family, 28, 32, 48, 52, 130
Kobra, Eduardo (artist), 175
Krätzeblock, 109, 118
Kugelmann, Yves, 170
Kugler, Victor (employee/helper), 69–73, 97, 99, 102
Kuiper, Maarten, 149, 150

L
Leopold, Ronald (executive director, Anne Frank House), 144, 175, 178, 183
Let Me Be Myself (portrait), 175
Levin, Meyer (novelist), 158, 162, 163
Liberation, by Allied troops
    hopes dashed, 103
    hopes for, 96, 103
Library books, 73, 76, 77
Liebe Kitty (Dear Kitty), 7, 159
Lyceum for Girls, 44, 50

M
Medical experimentation, 112–113
Mein Kampf (Hitler), 16, 17
Mengele, Dr. Josef, 110, 112–113
Merwedeplein ("The Merry") neighborhood, 46, 48, 156
    Anne's friends in, 60
    Frank family leaves, 69
Michael Frank Bank, 72
Mirren, Helen (actor), 164, 183
Moortje (pet cat), 69
Movie theaters, Jews banned from, 52

N

Nazis
    arrival in Amsterdam, 36–42
    mass murder by, estimated numbers, 30, 123
    rise and reach of, 16, 24–32, 35
Netherlands, Germany invades, 36–37
Nickname, at school, 49
Nussbaum, Laureen, 157, 159
    as author of *Shedding Our Stars*, 48, 52, 159
    correspondence with Otto, 159
    dissertation topic, 159
    friendship with Margot and Anne, 48–49
    on impact of Anne's diary, 6–7
    on *Liebe Kitty (Dear Kitty)* publication, 159
    Otto shares Anne's diary/writings with, 157, 159
    on Otto's search for family, 130–131
    on posthumous editing of Anne's writings, 159
    on what Anne might have become, 185
Nussbaum, Rudi, 7, 130–131, 137, 159

O

Occupants, Secret Annex
    activities during silent times, 76
    betrayal of, 140–151
    fates of, 132–133, 157
    personalities of, 75–76
    tensions between, 82–83
Opekta (business of Frank and van Pels), 66, 69
    building layout, 64–65
    burglaries at, 83, 96
    post-war operations, 99, 169
    salesmen's arrests, 145
Opekta employees, as helpers, 70–73

P

Pankoke, Vincent (investigator), 142–145
Pen pals, American, 34
Perkins, Millie (actor), 163, 164
Personality clashes, among Secret Annex occupants, 75–76, 83
Pfeffer, Fritz (dentist), 76, 77, 82, 83, 132
Plays, Anne writes/performs in, 52

Poland, German invasion/occupation of, 30, 38, 40
Polonsky, David (illustrator), 179
Pope John XXIII, 136
Portman, Natalie (actor), 164
The Princess with the Nose (children's play), 52
Prinsengracht (No. 263), 66–68. *See also* Anne Frank House; Secret Annex
    burglaries at, 83, 96
    demolition concerns, 169
    layout of, 84–85
    neighbors' suspicions about, 151
    Otto purchases, 169
    restoration of, 170
    view from, 151

R

Ration coupons, 72, 145
Reflection (painting), 180–181
Righteous Among the Nations (Israeli honor), 99
Rudashevski, Yitskhok, 6

S

Sacrifice, of helpers, 73
Scabies, 109, 118
Schepp, Jet (sculptor), 172
Schildkraut, Joseph (actor), 162, 164
Schloss, Eva (née Geiringer)
    memories of Anne, 46, 48, 49, 59
    Otto shares Anne's diary/writings with, 157, 159
    on Otto's desire to protect Anne, 158
    post-liberation encounter with Otto, 121, 126, 129
    as posthumous stepsister to Anne, 51, 136, 138
    preserves Otto's mission to memorialize Anne, 182
    on what Anne might have become, 180, 185
Secret Annex
    Anne's diary/writings retrieved from, 6, 156–157
    audio and virtual reality tours of, 175
    daily routine in, 77–78, 80–81
    daily visits from helpers, 73

dimensions and layout, 75, 84–85
entrance to, 64–65, 84, 85, 170
Fritz Pfeffer joins families in, 76
Gestapo raid on, 92–103
life in, 74–81
location of, 66
setting up, 70–71
settling into, 68, 69
tensions in, 82–83
van Pels family join Frank family in, 75
weekends in, 77, 81
Self-censorship, Anne's diary pages, 183
Shedding Our Stars (Nussbaum), 48, 52, 159
Silberbauer, Karl Josef (Gestapo agent), 94, 103, 142
   interactions with Miep Gies, 99, 105
Silberberg, Helmuth "Hello" [Ed], 60–6
The Silent Sister (Mizrahi), 91
Silent times, activities during, 76
Sleeping arrangements, Secret Annex, 75, 80, 84, 85
Star of David badges, 42
Stielau, Lothar, 158
Strasberg, Susan (actor), 162, 163
Straus Jr., Nathan, appeals on Frank family's behalf, 43
Studying, in Secret Annex, 76–77
"Subhumans," 30
Suijk, Cornelis, 158

T
Torture, 112–113
Typhus outbreak, 121

V
van Amerongen-Frankfoorder, Rachel, 121, 132
van Bladeren-Hartog, Lena, 146, 148

van Dijk, Ans, 149, 151
van Hall, Gijs (mayor of Amsterdam), 179
van Limburg Stirum, Otto, 165
van Maaren, Willem, 146, 147
van Maarsen, Jacqueline, 47, 50, 178, 179
van Pels, Auguste (wife of Hermann), 76, 82, 132
van Pels, Hermann (Otto's business partner), 66–69, 72, 132
van Pels, Peter (son of Hermann), 76, 82, 132–133
   Anne's comments on, 76, 77, 88–89
   Frank sisters' rivalry over, 86–91
   room in Secret Annex, 75, 84–85
van Pels family, interactions between, 82
van Wijk, Joop, 143–144, 150
Virtual reality tour, Secret Annex, 175
Voskuijl, Bep (employee/helper), 70, 71–72
   closeness with Anne, 73
   Gestapo raid and, 99
   name used by Margot, 171
   retrieves Anne's writings from secret annex, 6, 156–157
Voskuijl, Diny (sister of Bep), 144, 150
Voskuijl, Johan (father of Bep), 70
Voskuijl, Nelly (sister of Bep), 143, 146, 150

W
Weekends, in Secret Annex, 77, 81
Westerbork transit camp, 101, 103, 105
   last transport from, 108–109, 132
Weteringschans detention center, 95
Where is Anne Frank?, 179
Winters, Shelley (actor), 159, 163, 179

Z
Zapruder, Alexander, 6

PHOTO CREDITS

CENTENNIAL BOOKS

An Imprint of
Centennial Media, LLC
40 Worth St., 10th Floor
New York, NY 10013, U.S.A.

CENTENNIAL BOOKS is a trademark of Centennial Media, LLC

ISBN 978-1-951274-38-2

Distributed by
Simon & Schuster, Inc.
1230 Avenue of the Americas
New York, NY 10020, U.S.A.

For information about custom editions, special sales and premium and corporate purchases,
please contact Centennial Media at contact@centennialmedia.com.

Manufactured in China

10 9 8 7 6 5 4 3 2 1

Publishers & Co-Founders Ben Harris, Sebastian Raatz
Editorial Director Annabel Vered
Creative Director Jessica Power
Executive Editor Janet Giovanelli
Deputy Editors Ron Kelly, Alyssa Shaffer
Design Director Martin Elfers
Art Directors Olga Jakim,
Natali Suasnavas, Joseph Ulatowski
Copy / Production Patty Carroll, Angela Taormina
Assistant Art Director Jaclyn Loney
Photo Editor Jennifer Veiga
Production Manager Paul Rodina
Production Assistant Alyssa Swiderski
Editorial Assistant Tiana Schippa
Sales & Marketing Jeremy Nurnberg